What Others are Saying About This Book

"As a Christian having the privilege of reading this book, I can honestly say the author has 'hit the nail on the head.' If only everyone, Christians and non-Christians alike, could read this book. The book brings to awareness how necessary it is to help those around us become aware of the spiritual warfare that is trying to destroy the good all around us ... in our schools, TV, movies, sports, our family relationships, even in our churches. I highly recommend reading this book. Prayer is our strength. Pray—in Christ."

~P. Brown

"This book brings the truth of the Bible to our present-day American society. It is a book that gives the reader the unabashed position on explosive topics God speaks about in His Word. If the reader wants to know how to handle very controversial topics, in this day and time, read this book. God speaks, we understand."

~Elizabeth S.

"The author brings up a whole bunch of things that preachers don't preach about and Sunday school teachers don't teach about. But if you are a true believer, you need to know these things. This book goes deeper into more important topics than any other book I have read."

~Alan H.

THE BIBLE
VS
AMERICAN CULTURE

A Christian's Complete Guide to
the Enemy's Playbook

Case Olsen

Take A Stand Publishing
PO Box 1632
Montgomery, TX 77356

DEDICATION

Dedicated to the young believer who pronounced this to be "a book based on what God says, not the world's view."

And to those of her generation who will receive the teaching.

Published by Take A Stand Publishing, PO Box 1632, Montgomery, TX 77356

Published in the United States of America.

TABLE OF CONTENTS

FOREWORD

Many Christians will say, "Yes, I know there is a spiritual warfare going on," without quite realizing how widespread the warfare is, or how deeply the enemy has penetrated every area of our lives in America—even churches. There is a natural tendency to focus on specific issues that have affected one's own life the most, like abortion or racism or demonic possession. This book attempts to bring together a wide range of issues affecting the Christian, so the believer is not blindsided by attacks from one side while paying attention to a different side.

There is some implied criticism here of America's seminaries for not adequately preparing clergy with the biblical view in many subjects. One wonders: Have we American Christians been kept so safe that we have forgotten the blood of the martyrs—blood shed so we could receive the Bible as the true word of God? Have we become so enamored with academic scholarship that we have begun to compromise the testimony of the prophets and apostles?

The author is not out to "prove" anything in this book; there is no hidden agenda. The goal is simply to test American culture—both inside and outside the church—against the words of the Bible. The Bible does not pander to any human philosophy or cultural program. What it does do with infinite wisdom is equip Christians to "no longer be children, tossed to and fro and carried about with every wind of doctrine, by the cunning of men, by their craftiness in deceitful wiles" (Ephesians 4:14).

PART ONE

SEEING THE SIGNS

"You know how to interpret the appearance of the sky, but you cannot interpret the signs of the times" (Matthew 16:3).

In the Old Testament, the priests and prophets were sometimes referred to as watchmen. It was their job to warn the people whenever the people had strayed away from God and put themselves in danger from God's wrath.

In our time, the Christian clergy assume the mantle of Old Testament priests and prophets. It is their responsibility to see the signs of danger and warn us to avoid the danger. God regards the watchman's job with great seriousness. He tells the watchman: If "you do not speak to warn the wicked to turn from his way, that wicked man shall die in his iniquity, but his blood I will require at your hand" (Ezekiel 33:8). That is a severe warning—not only for the people, but for the watchman himself.

At the same time, we must all regard ourselves as watchmen.

In the New Testament, we read that Christ, through his shed blood, has "made us a kingdom, priests to his God and Father" (Revelation 1:6). So all believers are now considered equivalent to the Old Testament priests. If our clergy do not warn us, we are still responsible for acting as our own watchmen. We must train ourselves to interpret the signs of the times, so we can alert one another of danger.

1
DIALING 911 FOR PLANET EARTH

The Earth is in Danger, They Say

Elon Musk, the billionaire founder of several successful companies, has declared that humans need to become a multi-planet species by colonizing Mars. And, putting his money where his mouth is, he has started a company to make spaceships that will help achieve that goal. Musk's motivation seems to derive at least partly from the sheer excitement of exploration and discovery.

But he also is a player in a popular movement which maintains that planet earth has a fragile environment and might not support life much longer. Therefore, humans need an escape route, and Mars is the most likely destination. Leaders of this movement say that man-made climate change threatens to destroy our environment. Or an asteroid could suddenly strike from outer space and destroy all life. Or a series of storms on the surface of the sun could spew radiation that would blow away earth's atmosphere. Musk and others are issuing a 911 emergency call for an endangered planet earth, and they are depending upon science and technology to save us from the danger.

It's True, The Earth is in Danger

The prevailing view among the Mars enthusiasts is that there is no Creator God watching over the earth. We humans must fend for ourselves, they say, in a universe that has no soul. As they look out upon the universe, they see it as an unfeeling place, governed only by the laws of science and the law of chance.

The distance between this materialist view of the universe and the biblical view is greater even than the distance from earth to Mars. Many Christians, however, have become so comfortable with the scientific view that they fail to see its implications for their faith.

At the end of Moses' life, he summoned the people of Israel together to give them parting instructions. He reviewed for them everything God had done when God led them out of slavery in Egypt, and he reviewed everything God had said in giving them laws to live by. But his speech was not a simple recitation of history. As recorded in Deuteronomy 30:19–20, Moses began by saying, "I call heaven and earth to witness against you this day." Heaven was a "witness" because it was a real (though nonmaterial) place filled with spiritual (nonmaterial) beings— beings who were watching, and before whom humans could be held accountable.

Next Moses said, "I have set before you life and death, blessing and curse." According to Moses, life and death have nothing to do with whether we are a multi-planet species.

Life and death have to do with obeying God's commands. Moses concluded: "Therefore choose life, that you and your descendants may live, loving the LORD your God, obeying his voice, and cleaving to him" (Deuteronomy 30:19–20). This God in heaven is not just a God who gives commands, but is a God who loves us, and who demands that we love him and cleave to him (hold fast to him) in return.

Moses wrote with a sense of urgency which I would like to bring to the church in America. "Choose life," he said. This book is written with a sense that true teaching from God's word is not a matter of winning a debate, not a matter of listing differences of opinion or belief, but is a matter of life and death.

The world we live in is an amazing home for plant and animal and human life. But it is also home to unseen spiritual beings (Satan and his demons) who want to take us with them to a place of eternal destruction. They use deceptions and lies to draw us away from God. Living on Mars will not keep us safe from them. Nor will attending church on Sunday morning. Spiritual discernment, combined with the power of the risen Christ, is the only thing that will keep us safe. It is urgent that we learn to see through Satan's deceptions and choose life.

The Universe as a Giant Clock

Sir Isaac Newton was a scientist and also a devout Christian. He struggled to reconcile the strict cause and effect laws of nature with the Bible's picture of a God who rules over nature. His solution was to picture the universe as a complex machine which God set in motion at some initial time and then left to run on its own according to the laws of nature. It was as though God created a giant clock, wound it up, and left it ticking.

Newton's compromise leaves many stories in the Bible unexplained. For example, there is the story of Joshua calling on God to postpone sunset so his army could see to defeat the enemy army:

"Then spoke Joshua to the LORD in the day
when the LORD gave the Amorites over to the
men of Israel; and he said in the sight of Israel,

'Sun, stand thou still at Gibeon,
and thou Moon in the valley of Ai'jalon.'
And the sun stood still, and the moon stayed,
until the nation took vengeance on their
enemies.

Is this not written in the Book of Jashar? The
sun stayed in the midst of heaven, and did not
hasten to go down for about a whole day. There
has been no day like it before or since, when

the LORD hearkened to the voice of a man; for
the LORD fought for Israel"
(Joshua 10:12–14).

Here God interfered in the normal laws of nature. Part of the universe's clock stopped ticking for a whole day. Newton's compromise leaves us doubting that God is in control; it leaves us doubting that some parts of the Bible can be true.

In the book of Hebrews we read that Jesus "reflects the glory of God and bears the very stamp of his nature, upholding the universe by his word of power" (Hebrews 1:3). This means even normal, everyday events which we take for granted are dependent on Jesus' word of power to continue. The very air we breathe is supported by Jesus' word of power. God "makes his sun rise on the evil and on the good, and sends rain on the just and on the unjust" (Matthew 5:45).

There is a Plan

God created the heavens and the earth, and placed man on the earth. But he did not then sit back to watch and wait and see what would happen and what man would do. He had a plan, and over time he has revealed important parts of that plan to his servants the prophets, and to anyone able to see his hand at work in events of history. God said through the psalmist Asaph: "When the earth totters, and all its inhabitants, it is I who keep steady its pillars" (Psalm 75:3). If there ever should be an asteroid heading toward earth, it is God's asteroid; it did not come out of space by blind chance. The crises occurring across our country as natural disasters should open our eyes to the unfolding of God's plan—a plan in which God, by design, causes the earth to be shaken.

GOD ANNOUNCES PLAGUES

The book of Revelation contains prophecies of two long series of plagues—all caused by the action of angels sent from God. Here is a sentence describing one of those plagues:

> "The fourth angel poured his bowl on the sun, and it was allowed to scorch men with fire; men were scorched by the fierce heat, and they cursed the name of God who had power over these plagues, and they did not repent and give him glory" (Revelation 16:8–9).

The first part of that verse sounds like an article on the front page of today's newspaper, talking in ominous terms about the effects of climate change and global warming. And the second part of the prophecy accurately predicts what would certainly be missing from the modern newspaper article: namely, words of repentance.

In another plague described in Revelation, a third of the creatures of the sea are to die (Revelation 8:9)—a situation which we are witnessing in the world's oceans right now. Environmentalists and fishermen with firsthand experience vividly describe this phenomenon in news reports. According to Revelation, plagues like this are intended to get attention directed back to God in repentance. But it will be to no avail; the warning will be ignored by the majority of people, as prophesied in the following passage:

> "The rest of mankind, who were not killed by these plagues, did not repent of the works of their hands nor give up worshiping demons and idols of gold and silver and bronze and stone and wood, which cannot either see or hear or walk; nor did they repent of their murders or their sorceries or their immorality or their thefts" (Revelation 9:20–21).

Making the Connection

The signs are visible today: natural disasters of record-breaking proportions. And the words of prophecy are also there (in the Bible) for all to see. If our eyes are open, we can see there is a connection between events in the natural world and the God who made that world and who has ultimate control over that world.

A CALL TO REPENTANCE

But can we reconcile such events with the Bible's claim that God is "a God ready to forgive, gracious and merciful, slow to anger and abounding in steadfast love" (Nehemiah 9:17)? Can we call a God merciful who also allows disasters to occur? God is indeed "slow to anger," but at some point he says the evil is getting so out of hand that he must get our attention to call us to repentance.

When a third of the earth is burned up, and a third of the trees are burned up, and all grass is burned up (as described in Revelation 8:7, and as experienced in California), these disasters were planned by God before the beginning of time. God declared long ago that it must be so in order to draw our attention to him in repentance.

This is a time for watchmen to sound the trumpet. It is a time for watchmen to declare to their flock (and to the world) that man is *not* in control of the world. It is a time to declare that natural disasters are *not* simply a result of too many people driving SUV's and burning coal.

Barriers Christians Encounter

The biggest problem Christians in America face is a culture that is constantly redefining sin in whatever way suits it at the time, rather than in biblical terms. As a consequence, the biblical definition of sin has itself been declared to be sinful by cultural leaders. It has been declared sinful to tell expectant mothers they should not kill their babies in the womb. It has been declared sinful to object to any form of sexual deviance the LGBTQ people can invent. (LGBTQ, if you don't know, stands for Lesbian-Gay-Bisexual-Transgender-Queer, and is sometimes followed by a plus + sign to include any other deviant sexual identity someone may lay claim to.) It has been declared sinful to contradict the scientific "truth" of evolution. According to the prevailing cultural view, if anyone should repent, it is the Christians themselves!

WE BATTLE ENEMIES FROM WITHIN

A second problem faced by Bible-believing Christians is that many churches which call themselves Christian have compromised with the current cultural views. Therefore unbelievers looking at Christianity from the outside can say there really are some "good" Christians who have adopted "right" thinking. Christianity offers no challenge to them, no call to repentance. They can choose which brand of Christianity they like.

Those same churches which compromise with the culture also are likely to say that God only rescues, comforts, and uplifts. God would never cause wildfires or flooding, they say, because that is contrary to God's good and loving nature. Churches with such beliefs are no more likely to hear God's call to repentance than unbelievers.

BUT WE HAVE A RESPONSIBILITY

The difficulties don't remove Christians' responsibility to get the word out, to stand up and say, "Listen! God is speaking to us. Our sins are causing God's protection to be removed. The solution is not for us to become a multi-planet species, but for us to repent and turn to God."

Scripture warns us that most people may not hear the call. Scripture warns us that we will be mocked and scoffed at. But the evidence is there. It's in Scripture and in the news headlines. And it is the watchman's job to sound the trumpet.

2
GOD SPEAKS TO AMERICA

The Myth of "New Knowledge"

During a controversy at Baylor University in 2019, a newspaper editorial protested the refusal by the nominally Christian school to allow an LGBTQ group to register as an official campus activity. The article proclaimed twenty-first century Americans are now the proud possessors of "new knowledge" regarding homosexuality and gender fluidity, and therefore Baylor should be ashamed of itself for its regressive views. The author contrasted this new knowledge with "views once thought immutable" contained in "ancient scripture," and went on to assert confidently, "Gay America is here to stay." [*Dallas Morning News*, 6/5/2019, p. 14A, "Baylor backhands LGBTQ students," by Hal Wingo.]

Gay America may be here to stay, but there is nothing new about our knowledge of homosexuality. Our knowledge goes back to 2100 B.C., to the cities of Sodom and Gomorrah (whose existence is not only supported by "ancient Scripture" but by modern archeology). Knowledge also goes back to the lesbian Greek poet Sappho in the sixth century B.C., and to the moral decadence of the Roman emperors in the early centuries A.D. Knowledge about homosexuality and sexual deviance—and their consequences—is nothing new.

God Gives a Kind of New Knowledge

When God speaks directly to someone, the message comes as new knowledge—at least as far as that person is concerned. The substance of the message may be something the person could have deduced from reading the Bible, or perhaps heard more than once from Mom and Dad. But when a message comes directly from the Lord, it comes with a jolt, making the message personal and meaningful. It is what Job experienced when he heard God speak from the whirlwind. Job had been complaining bitterly to God for about thirty chapters in the book of Job, but after Job heard God's voice, he changed his tune. He said, "I had heard of thee by the hearing of the ear, but now my eye sees thee; therefore I despise myself, and repent in dust and ashes (Job 42:5–6).

God is speaking directly to America today to give us new knowledge. It is the same knowledge he gave his people thousands of years ago, but it comes to us as "new" because it comes with power and immediacy. It wakes us up to realize God is present, he is the same, and he brooks no violation of his law.

No matter how many times and how forcefully God speaks, however, we are quite capable of shutting him out and refusing to listen to him. The Bible records many instances of God's people refusing to hear him and hardening their hearts against him. One such instance is described in 2 Chronicles 33:10, which speaks of Manasseh the king in Jerusalem: "The LORD spoke to Manasseh and to his people, but they gave no heed." The LORD had spoken to Manasseh and his people many times, over many years, but they refused to listen.

GOD SPEAKS THROUGH HISTORICAL EVENTS

The Bible contains God's rules for his people, but it also contains accounts of God speaking to his people through historical events. The incident about Manasseh is an example. Here is the complete paragraph from which that quote was taken:

> "The LORD spoke to Manasseh and to his people, but they gave no heed. Therefore the LORD brought upon them the commanders of the army of the king of Assyria, who took Manasseh with hooks and bound him with fetters of bronze and brought him to Babylon. And when he was in distress he entreated the favor of the LORD his God and humbled himself greatly before the God of his fathers. He prayed to him, and God received his entreaty and heard his supplication and brought him again to Jerusalem into his kingdom. Then Manasseh knew that the LORD was God" (2 Chronicles 33:10–13).

The prophet's words were initially discounted by Manasseh. It wasn't until God sent the king of Assyria with his army to take strong action against Manasseh, that Manasseh paid attention.

Over the years, the Lord also spoke to his people through natural disasters like famine and disease. For example, even though the prophet Jeremiah warned the people against their sinful living, the people would not listen. Finally, Jeremiah records the Lord's endgame:

> "The LORD said to me: 'Do not pray for the welfare of this people. Though they fast, I will not hear their cry, and though they offer burnt offering and cereal offering, I will not accept them; but I will consume them by the sword, by famine, and by pestilence'" (Jeremiah 14:11–12).

And God did as he promised: He spoke to the people by the sword, by famine, and by pestilence.

God is speaking to America today. The voices of any people who speak God's message against the LGBTQ movement (for one example) are being forcibly suppressed. (In this chapter I use the LGBTQ movement as an example of America's moral rebellion, but it is only the most recent example.) And when the message does get through, the messenger is blamed. God is kept out of the picture.

Yet God continues speaking through "natural" events. And just as in Bible times, when the message is not received, God patiently repeats it, waiting for his people to turn to him in repentance.

God Speaks Through Natural Disasters

The Bible contains several examples of God speaking to his people through natural disasters. He used his prophets to explain to the people that he was calling on them to repent. The words God spoke through Amos provide one example:

> "'And I also withheld the rain from you when there were yet three months to the harvest; I would send rain upon one city, and send no rain upon another city; one field would be rained upon, and the field on which it did not rain withered; so two or three cities wandered to one city to drink water, and were not satisfied; yet you did not return to me,' says the LORD" (Amos 4:7–8).

GOD SPEAKS TO NEW ORLEANS THROUGH HURRICANE KATRINA, 2005

New Orleans has achieved a proud image of libertinism over its history, but in recent years has added onto that image with its welcoming of the LGBTQ movement. It has been such a long time that God's laws seem old and forgotten about. But God has told us, "I the LORD do not change" (Malachi 3:6). God is calling on New Orleans to repent and change their ways before it is too late.

GOD SPEAKS TO NEW YORK THROUGH HURRICANE SANDY, 2012

New York has achieved the distinction (probably a record-breaking distinction) of killing a third of its babies through abortion. Put in biblical terms, New York is sacrificing a third of its children as burnt offerings on the altar of lust, which is an abomination to God. God also sees New York's whole-hearted adoption of the LGBTQ abominations, and is bringing the city's guilt to remembrance.

GOD SPEAKS TO HOUSTON THROUGH HURRICANE HARVEY, 2017

Houston proudly and defiantly elected for three terms a lesbian mayor who attempted to stop Christian preachers from teaching God's laws about sexuality. God sees Houston and brings their guilt to remembrance.

GOD SPEAKS TO CALIFORNIA THROUGH WILDFIRES, 2007 TO ???

California has led the nation—in fact, led the world—in championing the LGBTQ cause. While California has embraced all people who burn with unnatural desire, God has in turn allowed a large portion of the state to burn to ashes. God sees, and brings California's guilt to remembrance.

"SWEEPING AWAY OF MOIST AND DRY ALIKE"

When you read the above paragraphs, you may protest that there were many people in these places who had no involvement in the LGBTQ movement, or the abortion industry, and yet the disasters affected them equally. You may think, if these disasters were from God, surely God would have singled out the worst offenders and left all others alone.

In the book of Deuteronomy, Moses warns the people "lest there be among you … one who, when he hears the words of this sworn covenant, blesses himself in his heart, saying, 'I shall be safe, though I walk in the stubbornness of my heart'" (Deuteronomy 29:19). Moses instructs the *entire community* to watch out for any person who said, "I can disobey God's laws, and nothing will happen, because God does not see." Then Moses adds these words: "This would lead to the sweeping away of moist and dry alike" (Deuteronomy 29:19). Moses warned that all would suffer the consequences of a single person's sin if the people allowed sin to grow and fester among them.

God Speaks to All of America

What about the floods affecting the farmlands in middle America? What does God have against all those farmers?

Flooding of farmlands not only affects farmers, it reduces our food supply. Hurricanes Katrina, Sandy, and Harvey touched many people besides the cities mentioned. Through these events, God speaks to *all* Americans, and warns about our leaders' promotion of the unspeakable abominations of the LGBTQ movement. It will lead "to the sweeping away of moist and dry alike." The warning touches everyone. No one is safe. God wants us to find leaders—not just in government, but in businesses and churches and health services—who will stand for God's laws. He brings our disobedience to remembrance before the eyes of all, and calls on us to repent and change our ways. He calls us to turn to God *in truth* before it is too late.

A WARNING FROM "ANCIENT SCRIPTURE"

The author of the book of Chronicles looks back at the disasters God sent against his people, and summarizes many years of history this way:

> "The LORD, the God of their fathers, sent
> persistently to them by his messengers, because
> he had compassion on his people and on his
> dwelling place; but they kept mocking the
> messengers of God, despising his words, and

scoffing at his prophets, till the wrath of the LORD rose against his people, till there was no remedy" (2 Chronicles 36:15–16).

God spoke to his people, not out of malice, but out of compassion. He wanted his people to look ahead, to see the consequences of acting against God's laws. But what was their reaction? They mocked, they despised, they scoffed ... until there was no remedy.

Will people in America continue to mock, and despise, and scoff ... until there is no remedy? And will the church be discerning enough to see, and bold enough to declare, God's message to us?

3
THE CORONAVIRUS

Yes, God Can Speak Through a Disease

Sometimes the claim is made—by Christians—that a disease like the coronavirus has nothing to do with God, because God only does good and never evil. But the Bible has numerous examples of God using a disease to give his people a message.

When King David sinned against the Lord by killing Uriah to take Uriah's wife, the Bible tells us, "And the LORD afflicted the child that Uriah's wife bore to David, and he became sick" (2 Samuel 12:15). The Lord sent David a message that his sin against the Lord was serious.

An example from the New Testament is the time when Herod delivered an oration and the people called out to him, "The voice of a god, and not of a man." The Bible says, "Immediately an angel of the LORD struck him down, because he did not give God the glory, and he was eaten by worms and breathed his last" (Acts 12:22–23). Through a deadly disease, the LORD sent Herod and the people who worshiped him a message that man was not to take God's glory upon himself.

HAS GOD SPOKEN TO AMERICA THROUGH THE CORONAVIRUS?

It falls to believers—Christians—to proclaim the answer to this question. No one else is listening to God's voice. Too often, no one *wants* to hear God's voice. At the height of the pandemic, *Time* magazine published an issue titled "Finding Hope." (4/27/2020). In 104 pages *Time* printed interviews with many people whom they considered important in America. There were examples of courage and human strength in the face of danger, but God was never mentioned. The only "religious" person interviewed was the Dalai Lama, a Buddhist.

God has put Christians on earth for a purpose: to proclaim his truth when no one else will.

GOD GETS OUR ATTENTION

Before God can speak to us he must get our attention.

His job is easier said than done in America. We're a society that goes at a frantic pace: work, sports, school, yoga class, soccer match, work, shopping, school, travel—then repeat in rapid succession. Sunday has become NFL football day. Some Christians go to church on Sunday morning and schedule Sunday afternoon for grocery shopping. The Sabbath for many believers has become a half day instead of a whole day.

One weekday afternoon during the coronavirus crisis, I was walking in my neighborhood and noticed people were walking their dogs in the middle of the street because there was no traffic. I said, "This feels peaceful, almost like Sabbath day." Then it occurred to me how the Lord dealt with his disobedient people in the Old Testament: He deported them to another country so the land could "enjoy its Sabbaths." While his people were frantically occupied seven days a week, they never gave the land a rest. The Lord warned Moses in advance that this would happen. He said, "But the land shall be left by them, and enjoy its Sabbaths while it lies desolate without them; and they shall make amends for their iniquity, because they spurned my ordinances, and their soul abhorred my statutes" (Leviticus 26:43).

Through the coronavirus, the Lord for a time forced America to slow down, to cease its constant bedlam, so that his voice might be heard.

God's Message

During the pandemic I received emails from Christian organizations saying, "Everybody please pray. Pray for an end to this crisis. Pray for a cure to be found for this virus. Pray that God will protect us."

It is always right to turn to God in prayer, but prayer involves listening as well as speaking. What is God saying? They missed the point. As far as they are concerned, God has nothing to do with any disease outbreak. This virus can only come from Satan, so we need to call on God to defeat Satan. They forget that nothing happens apart from the permissive will of God.

Fasting and praying without listening to God's voice was a mistake made by God's people in the time of Jeremiah the prophet. God told Jeremiah: "Though they fast, I will not hear their cry, and though they offer burnt offering and cereal offering I will not accept them; but I will consume them by the sword, by famine, and by pestilence" (Jeremiah 14:12). Fasting and praying were of no avail if the people remained stubborn and persisted in their disobedience to God. The people might cry out to God, but the pestilence would still come to them because of their steadfast refusal to obey God's laws. God wanted not only prayer, he wanted obedience.

4
AMERICA'S ABOMINATIONS

Strike Three Called

We may stack our lineup with supposed heavy-hitters, but God is the umpire, and he has called strike three. America has struck out. The three strikes against America are three abominations which America has not only permitted, but from the seat of government power has promoted and sponsored.

An abomination is a human behavior which the Lord God regards as appallingly evil—you might even say evil beyond "ordinary" evils. Since America has encoded several abominations into its laws, it can be said that these truly are *American* abominations. We will list below the three official abominations—the three strikes against us—in historical sequence.

Abomination #1—the Idolatry of Science

U.S. courts have ruled public schools cannot teach that the natural world was created and is sustained by God, since such teaching would constitute an establishment of religion by the government. What is taught instead is a completely materialistic view of the universe—a view in which everything is explained as resulting from the big bang and from evolution. In other words, the teaching of science—teaching performed by people created by God, for the benefit of students created by God, about all the things around them created by God—can never be allowed to mention God.

Many books have been written on the subject of science and religion, but for the Christian, a couple of basic facts stand out.

Concerning the big bang theory: Remember that the brilliant astrophysicist with equations written all over his blackboard describing the effects of the big bang cannot explain where the big bang came from. He takes it for granted that it arose from natural causes (no help from God), but he has no idea what those causes might be. He casually gives the universe credit for creating itself.

Concerning evolution: Remember that the most expert biologist, using a modern lab and all the organic chemicals which might have existed in a "primordial soup," cannot create a living thing. And yet he assumes life sprang by chance from such a primordial soup. He is in effect saying molecules in a swamp, interacting randomly with one another, are smarter than he is.

These scientists have made nature into a god. They attribute to nature miraculous powers and knowledge far beyond human power and knowledge, and they do obeisance to it. Their idol is nature, and they are engaged in false idol worship. As the apostle Paul said, they have "exchanged the truth about God for a lie and worshiped and served the creature rather than the Creator" (Romans 1:25).

And they cling to this idolatry because, as high priests of their religion, it allows them to claim power and prestige for themselves. The places of worship for these priests are our schools, especially colleges and universities. America has a law against the establishment of a state religion, but we have established a state religion of science, and by law our schools must teach it.

Science seems to satisfy many requirement of a religion. Science comes to our rescue when a new disease strikes by giving us the technology to develop antidotes and vaccines. Science gives us the means to see into the future when something like climate change occurs. And science explains what we must do to survive the changes. In short, science says we don't need God anymore. Science has replaced God.

Christians, we need to pray that our children will be protected from worshiping the false god of science. Christian parents need to take responsibility for teaching their children the truth about God, and for teaching them to give God the glory for his creation. (The Psalms are a wonderful source of instruction here.) And we need to pray that the blinders will be removed from the eyes of those working and teaching in the scientific world, so they may repent and turn from worshiping the creature rather than the Creator.

Abomination #2—Infanticide

The Bible lists the practice of burning children as an offering to a god—infanticide—as one of the ancient abominations God condemned. King Ahaz, for example, is described as having "burned his sons as an offering, according to the *abominable practices* of the nations whom the LORD drove out before the people of Israel" (2 Chronicles 28:3 emphasis mine). The modern equivalent is the practice of abortion, the offering of one's children to the god of lust.

Christian prayers and actions against abortion seem to have been more unified and effective in recent years than those against the idolatry of science. The number of abortion centers in some states in America has been reduced. The fight against abortion has been aided by the availability of sonograms, which show the human fetus as a living, moving, sentient being. The pictures provide physical evidence to demonstrate the horror of killing a baby.

Christians should take heart from seeing the initial results of their prayers against this abomination and realize that their prayers are having an effect. Abortion, however, continues to be a "constitutional right" in the eyes of our courts, and our government continues to subsidize abortions (through Medicaid reimbursements to Planned Parenthood). What we can do: pray that our country will repent and turn away from the abomination of abortion. And let those who are able donate time and resources to pro-life pregnancy centers.

Abomination #3—Homosexuality and Sexual Immorality

Judges in America have now declared that based on the U.S. Constitution, homosexuals have a right to marry one another. How did this come about, since the Constitution does not mention marriage?

Satan came up with a clever ploy: *Equality* was made central to discussions involving sexual morality. In America, the debate has successfully been turned from whether homosexuality is moral to whether homosexuals should be granted marriage equality. Americans, including Christians, seem to have fallen for the sly switcheroo, and have forgotten that the Bible says bluntly that homosexuality is an abomination. God commanded his people: "You shall not lie with a male as with a woman; *it is an abomination*" (Leviticus 18:22 emphasis mine). And in the New Testament, Paul agreed with that statement, and said homosexual behavior should not be permitted in the Christian church.

There is also a tendency to minimize the seriousness of homosexual behavior because there is not always an obvious victim. Abortions have a clear victim: a helpless, innocent baby murdered in its mother's womb. But homosexual activity does not always appear to victimize an innocent person. There is a temptation to say sexual immorality is a personal matter between consenting adults and has no effect on anything or anyone else. Or we may add it is also a personal matter between an individual and God, but doesn't affect the rest of us. This uncertain attitude weakens Christian prayers and Christian voices. We need our prayers to be strong against the abomination of homosexuality.

And we need to know that all sexual immorality, including homosexual activity, has a victim. We know that people who engage in sexual immorality may become victims of STDs, but there is also another—unexpected—victim.

AN UNEXPECTED VICTIM OF SEXUAL IMMORALITY

The Bible tells us when sexual immorality occurs in private between consenting adults and nobody seems to get hurt, there is still a victim: *the land*. The Lord said to the people of Israel, through Moses: "But you shall keep my statutes and my ordinances and do none of these abominations, either the native or the stranger who sojourns among you ... *lest the land vomit you out, when you defile it, as it vomited out the nation that was before you*" (Leviticus 18:26, 28 emphasis mine). And the Lord said later through the prophet Jeremiah:

> "By the waysides you have sat awaiting lovers
> like an Arab in the wilderness. You have
> *polluted the land* with your vile harlotry"
> (Jeremiah 3:2 emphasis mine).

The land itself was polluted by the people's sexual immorality, and today we likewise are polluting our land—the land we love, the land of the free and home of the brave—with our sexual immorality. People concerned about modern climate change should take notice here: The Lord is not telling us today that our land has been polluted by fossil fuels; he is telling us that our land has been polluted by sexual immorality. In Jeremiah, the Lord went on to tell how the land suffered *devastating climate change* because of its moral pollution:

> "Therefore the showers have been withheld,
> and the spring rain has not come; yet you have
> a harlot's brow, you refuse to be ashamed"
> (Jeremiah 3:3).

THE NEW MEANING OF PRIDE

The new meaning of pride (according to the gay culture) is *defiance*. Pride is no longer satisfaction at a job well done. It is an angry shout-out to Christians to "take your Christian morality and shove it."

The LGBTQ community sponsors PRIDE events to promote their lifestyle in the public eye. But those events are not about pride, in the usual sense. They are about *refusing to be ashamed*, as Jeremiah puts it—refusing to accept the verdict of the Bible. They are declaring war against anyone who dares to proclaim God's true word, and they have gained strong allies in all segments of society, including within the church itself.

But God sees them, and God sees America's openness and active consent to their lifestyle. And according to God's word, the more we refuse to be ashamed of our sexual immorality, the more we are polluting the land. There will come a tipping point when the land will simply "vomit us out."

The Abomination Spoken of by the Prophet Daniel

The prophet Daniel spoke of a time (see Daniel 11:31 and 12:11) when "the abomination that makes desolate is set up" (set up in the place where God was to be worshiped, that is). In the Bible, "desolate" means childless. We know childlessness was not God's intention for mankind, because when he created Adam and Eve he told them to "be fruitful and multiply, and fill the earth and subdue it" (Genesis 1:28). Satan likes childlessness, because if children are never born then he doesn't have to go to the trouble of destroying them. Homosexuality, of course, stands in biological opposition to human reproduction. Homosexuality is an abomination that makes desolate, and we see it now established in places that bear God's name, places that are supposed to be for worship of God.

I have in front of me a February 2020 news clipping with an announcement that has become fairly typical for our time. It announces that Bishop Bonnie Perry is to be the first female and openly gay bishop of the Michigan diocese of the Episcopal Church. A photograph shows Bishop Perry standing in her church near the altar with hands folded, smiling sweetly like a schoolgirl who has just won the county spelling bee. *What could be more innocent?* We are encouraged to let down our guard and go our way. Let them "do their thing" if they want. It can't do us any harm.

But Jesus said otherwise. Jesus tells us to take heed of Daniel's prophecy.

"So when you see the desolating sacrilege spoken of by the prophet Daniel, standing in the holy place (let the reader understand), then let those who are in Judea flee to the mountains; let him who is on the housetop not go down to take what is in his house; and let him who is in the field not turn back to take his mantle. And alas for those who are with child and for those who give suck in those days! Pray that your flight may not be in winter or on a sabbath. For then there will be great tribulation, such as has not been from the beginning of the world until now, no, and never will be. And if those days had not been shortened, no human being would be saved; but for the sake of the elect those days will be shortened" (Matthew 24:15–22).

We are today seeing a desolating sacrilege standing in the holy place. Does Jesus say we can safely ignore it? No, Jesus said for us to flee because this is a sign of big trouble ahead. Jesus said for us to take warning because a terrible abomination—a deadly spiritual virus—has even infected his church, the body of Christ. What to do? He tells us: "Come out of her, my people, lest you take part in her sins, lest you share in her plagues" (Revelation 18:4). If our local church, or the denomination our church sends money to, takes part in such sins, we are to leave it in a hurry and not look back.

LEARNING FROM THE CITY OF SODOM

Homosexual behavior is referred to as sodomy, named after the city of Sodom mentioned in the book of Genesis. The Bible tells us that God sent two angels, in the form of men, to investigate the reports he had heard of wickedness in the city of Sodom. When the angels arrived at Sodom, the men of the city surrounded the house where the angels were staying and demanded to "know them" (that is, rape them homosexually). But the angels struck the men of the city with blindness so they could not carry out their immoral intentions. Then the angels warned the one righteous family found in the city—the family of Lot—to run away and escape, because the Lord was going to destroy the city. They told Lot's family: "Flee for your life; do not look back or stop anywhere in the valley; flee to the hills, lest you be consumed" (Genesis 19:17).

Does the angels' command sound familiar? It is exactly what Jesus has also told us to do: flee, lest we be consumed.

The fate of Sodom was destruction. "Then the LORD rained on Sodom and Gomorrah brimstone and fire from the LORD out of heaven; and he overthrew those cities, and all the valley, and all the inhabitants of the cities, and what grew on the ground" (Genesis 19:24–25). Our modern, scientific minds may try to visualize this destruction as something like a small volcano springing up out of the ground and raining fire down on the cities. We can't imagine fire and brimstone actually falling on Sodom *from heaven*. But we will see in upcoming sections of this message it is logical that the fire should come from heaven. The evil of sodomy has repercussions in heaven and on earth. The wickedness of Sodom caused the pillars of heaven to shake, so that heaven itself had to react.

THE UNITED METHODIST CONFERENCE OF 2019

In February 2019 the United Methodist Church held a worldwide conference in St. Louis, where they voted on whether to recognize same-sex marriage and ordination of LGBTQ clergy. The vote was 438 to 384 against such recognition. There were active church members present who were openly homosexual or lesbian, and they wanted their church to take the next step in promoting the LGBTQ agenda.

What an American solution to a problem this was: take a vote! "Some people have this point of view, and some people have the other point of view, so we'll vote and go with the majority." But neither Satan nor God runs a democracy. They run *king*-doms, and we are all members of either the one kingdom or the other. There is no tallying of votes.

When their church began admitting homosexual church members, those Methodists who knew the Bible should have run as fast as they could to get away. They should have fled to the hills (left the church which was compromising on sexual morality) and not looked back. That is the response God has said we must make if we want to survive the times.

Pray Against America's Abominations

We need to pray that the blood of Jesus will cut off the idolatry of science, the infanticide of abortion, and the sexual immorality of the LGBTQ movement.

And let us pray that our children's minds will be protected from these abominations so that they may be drawn closer to God, rather than lured away from him.

Nothing New Under the Sun

The Preacher said: "What has been is what will be, and what has been done is what will be done; and there is nothing new under the sun" (Ecclesiastes 1:9).

Skeptics may dismiss the Bible as ancient mythology, but the writers of 2,000 and 3,000 years ago were writing—under God's guidance—about us. Idol worship, infanticide, sexual immorality (including what was referred to then as "male cult prostitutes"), were prevalent in ancient society, and they are now prevailing in American society, as well. Truly, there is nothing new under the sun.

Can America turn from its abominations before the land that we love "vomits us out" in complete revulsion?

5
MAGIC AND SORCERY ARE WITH US AND AMONG US

Author's note: This chapter may be the most important chapter in our book, because the subject matter is the least-discussed in churches and seminaries.

The Prince of the Power of the Air

In his letter to the Ephesians, Paul refers to Satan as the prince of the power of the air. He tells the Ephesians: "And you he made alive, when you were dead through the trespasses and sins in which you once walked, following the course of this world, following the prince of the power of the air, the spirit that is now at work in the sons of disobedience" (Ephesians 2:1–2). And later in the same letter, Paul says we are battling "against the spiritual forces of evil in the heavenly places" (Ephesians 6:12).

We cannot see these forces with our human eyes, so we need spiritual insight to be aware of their stratagems. Though we cannot see these forces, we cannot ignore them. The Bible says we are not to sit complacently in neutral territory, but we are to enter the spiritual battle as the people of Israel were instructed to enter the land of Canaan: "by thrusting out all your enemies from before you" (Deuteronomy 6:19).

SATAN THE MASTER LIAR

American churches tend not to take the Bible's admonitions against magic, sorcery, and astrology seriously. I've never heard a minister warn his congregation not to read the daily horoscope in the newspaper, or not to laugh over the fortune cookies at the local Chinese restaurant, or not to visit the palm reader at the county fair. These activities seem harmless, light entertainment, yet each one tempts demonic spirits to take control over us—like that first cigarette that the lung cancer victim once smoked.

The Bible never says it is okay to participate in fortune telling "as long as it is just for fun." The Bible simply says don't do it. The same goes for hypnotism, automatic writing, séances, and Ouija boards. God's word tells us not to engage in these practices nor form friendships based on a person's Zodiac sign. All these activities invite involvement with demonic powers which are stronger than we are. Satan, the pre-eminent liar and deceiver, is behind them all. His technique is still the same as it was in the Garden of Eden with Eve. He first asks, "Did God say so and so?" to plant a seed of doubt. Then he continues, "Well, let me tell you, God was just trying to keep you from something good, from something fun. So in this case you're better off just ignoring him."

DEMONS ARE REAL

Demons are invisible to us. Their existence is denied or ignored by science, but the results of their activity are visible in human behavior. Demons are stronger than we are. Human flesh cannot defeat Satan and his army of demons. The only power that is stronger than Satan is the power of the name of Jesus. Christians—those who know the salvation of the Lord Jesus Christ—have been entrusted with this power. Christians alone may pronounce the name of Jesus against Satan's demons. This puts Christians at the center of the cosmic battle between good and evil. And it means Satan is very happy when Christians remain ignorant of the power they've been given.

Incidentally, the currently popular idea of "binding" demons is not biblical. Jesus already "bound" Satan with his death on the cross. The Bible tells us that demons are to be *cast out*, not bound. This may seem like a small point, but small things can change the outcome of a large battle. Also note that demons cannot be cast out with so-called holy water or by waving a crucifix. Only the name of Jesus Christ is powerful enough to cast out demons.

The Spirit of Jesus must be present in the person invoking Jesus' name. The Bible tells about seven sons of a Jewish high priest named Sceva who invoked the name of Jesus over a man possessed by a demon, but "the evil spirit answered them, 'Jesus I know, and Paul I know; but who are you?' And the man in whom the evil spirit was leaped on them, mastered all of them, and overpowered them, so that they fled out of that house naked and wounded" (Acts 19:15–16). Demons and their power are real, but the power of Jesus is greater.

Passive Mind Techniques

Satan and his demons see a passive mind as an invitation to enter and take control. For example, a passive mind is necessary for hypnotism to take place. When a hypnotist says "relax," "you are feeling sleepy," "watch the pendulum go back and forth ... back and forth ... back and forth," he wants to create in his subject a completely passive mind that can be controlled by outside spirits.

Various meditation techniques like Transcendental Meditation rely on creating a passive mind, which can then be taken over by demonic powers. "Mindfulness meditation" is promoted by major healthcare organizations such as United Health Care. No doubt the insurers see themselves as offering "progressive" health care, and would scoff at the suggestion that they were creating a gateway for demons. But mindfulness meditation, when carried to its logical conclusion, is a form of self-hypnotism—one allows oneself to be placed under the control of an outside spirit.

Some forms of meditation involve monotonous repetition of a word or phrase known as a mantra. Saying a mantra over and over again has an effect similar to focusing on a pendulum going back and forth: It causes a passive mind and invites demonic powers to enter one's mind. Once again, ministers need to speak out. Our watchmen need to wake up and warn all their unsuspecting lay people.

Concentration

Here the word "concentration" is being used not in the sense of thinking hard about a difficult subject, but in the sense of focusing thoughts—spirits—in a powerful way on a single point.

Concentration on a word (a technique used in karate) or concentration on a point in a picture, are techniques used to summon demonic powers to a location. The voodoo doll is an example of the use of focused thought or concentration. The person using the doll associates the doll with some other person, then puts a pin in a spot on the doll where he would like to send some power of the air (a demon) to affect that person. The pin is only an indicator of where the concentrated thought is to be focused. So, for example, if the voodooist wants to cause a headache in another person, he puts a pin in the head and focuses all his thought on sending a demon to cause a headache in that other person.

Acupuncture—a medical treatment from China that also uses pins—is coming into common use in America. When you take an acupuncture treatment, you make yourself into a voodoo doll. The acupuncture practitioner applies pins to parts of your body where you may want pain relief and then focuses thoughts on those pins. Of course, the treatment is advertised as being "only for good, only for helping." But demons are demons. Once you let them in, they cannot be controlled by human means. They can only be cast out by the power of Jesus' name. They may at first deceive you into thinking they are doing good, but like Satan himself, they are liars and deceivers.

Notice these two similar techniques come from opposite sides of the globe. Acupuncture comes from China and voodoo from Africa and the Caribbean, but they both use pins and focused thoughts to direct demonic powers to specific parts of the body. It shows the universality of Satan's influence and the universality of human willingness to tap into demonic power.

Eastern Religions

Eastern religious teaching has become especially prominent in American culture in recent years. Not only have mindfulness meditation and acupuncture become accepted by major healthcare institutions, but yoga and tai chi classes have been established in many churches and church-sponsored institutions like assisted living centers. Defenders of such classes will say about yoga, "It's just stretching." But why not do ordinary stretching exercises, if that is the case? And they will say about tai chi, "It's just gentle calisthenics." But why not do ordinary calisthenics, if that is the case? In both cases, the answer is because there is something different in tai chi and yoga than in ordinary exercises. The something different is the invocation of unseen powers of the air.

Martial arts from Eastern cultures all attempt to invoke "powers of the air"—which are, in fact, demons. Karate, yoga, tai chi, judo, jujitsu: all call on demonic powers through focused thoughts. These powers may be invisible, but they are real. Satan has cleverly removed any understanding of demonic forces from our religious training in seminaries. Ministers without such knowledge cannot warn us of the dangers.

Circles in Witchcraft

The circle has significance both in witchcraft and in Eastern religions. Now, you may wonder if we should really take this idea seriously. After all, a circle is a perfectly harmless and everyday shape. Circles are everywhere, from the wheels on our cars to the dinner plates on our tables. Recall, however, that the pin also is a harmless everyday object, but as we have noticed, it can become the focus for demon activity when used in voodoo or acupuncture. The difference comes when it is a focal point for thoughts (demons).

Sometimes the public explanation given for the circle's significance in occult teaching is that it represents completeness or wholeness. Completeness and wholeness sound like innocent concepts, but these are versions of completeness and wholeness which completely exclude God. They are closely linked to an idea of a universal brotherhood of man—a brotherhood (or wholeness) that exists (they claim) apart from repentance and the salvation of Jesus Christ.

In Eastern religions such as Taoism, a circle may stand for the entire universe. The South Korean flag shows an example of this. At the center of the flag is a circle representing the universe, and shaded areas within the circle representing the yin and yang from which everything in the universe is supposed to have emanated.

Historically, the circle has represented the sun in various pagan religions and been the focus of sun worship. (The Egyptian sun god Ra was no doubt one of the gods the Lord brought judgment upon at the first Passover. At Exodus 12:12 the Lord told Moses: "For I will pass through the land of Egypt that night, and I will smite all the first-born in the land of Egypt, both man and beast; and on all the gods of Egypt I will execute judgments: I am the LORD." My guess is that the next morning the Egyptians found that all the circles they used to represent the god Ra had been defaced or destroyed.)

One symbol used prominently in sorcery is called the solar cross, which consists of a circle divided into four quadrants by vertical and horizontal lines, like the crosshairs in a telescopic sight.

From ancient times the circle in the solar cross has represented the sun—a source of power—and the point where the lines cross at the center of the circle has been a point of focus for the powers of the air.

I know of at least one Christian organization which uses the solar cross as their logo. How did they come up with this symbol? The cross in the circle is obviously not a Christian cross since its horizontal and vertical lines are of equal length. Does this organization have any idea what they are doing? One can only wonder.

Do We Need to Form Circles to Pray?

A standard ritual in some Christian families is for everyone to stand in a circle and hold hands to pray before a meal. Christians should know this is how witches pray before a coven ceremony. Witches stand in a circle to focus power—the power of spirits of the air—into the center of their circle. The perimeter of the circle is also thought to protect them from "alien" powers, like the power of Christians' prayers coming against their evil purposes. If there is a break in the perimeter, they warn, it could let in those alien powers. (We know, however, the power of Jesus is stronger than any power witches may call upon.)

In Christian groups, there is sometimes a sense that prayer cannot begin until everyone has joined in the circle and everyone is holding hands with the next person. I have even heard voices say, "Don't let the circle be broken." They are unconsciously subscribing to the witches' idea of concentrating power at an area of focus: an idea which is effective for summoning spirits of the air (demons), but not for invoking the Holy Spirit of God. The idea of holding hands in a circle to pray appears nowhere in the Bible. If you say, "But it is just a way of our feeling unity in our family," all I can tell you is God would be pleased if you would continue to pray, but get rid of the "unbroken circle" idea.

The Pyramid and the All-Seeing Eye

The pyramid on our dollar bills, along with the all-seeing eye at its top, are occult symbols, but these symbols are usually dismissed as quaint artifacts of antiquity with no modern relevance. But these symbols are part of modern Freemasonry and should give us pause whenever we see them. The pyramid hearkens back to the days of Pharaoh's magicians in Egypt, who had true magical powers, not just sleight-of-hand capability. (Recall how Pharaoh's magicians could change a staff into a serpent and the waters of the Nile into blood, in imitation of the Lord's miracles.) The public explanation given for the all-seeing eye is that it represents protection under the eye of God. But the eye represents the authority of a god other than the God of the Bible: an authority that wants to rule over us in place of the true God. (Masons assume they will be favored sons of this false god because of their secret and blasphemous rituals.)

Pentagrams

The pentagram—especially the pentagram with two points going up and one point going straight down—is used among occultists and sorcerers as a symbol of Satan. In various cultures the pentagram has been thought to have magic powers. So why, then, is the pentagram in such popular use by Christians to represent stars at Christmas time? Christians need to be aware and awake. Ministers need to speak out.

Hexagrams

You have probably heard the expression "to put a hex on someone." The word hex is a reference to the hexagram: a six-pointed star composed of two superimposed equilateral triangles, one triangle pointing up, and the other pointing down. The hexagram is one of the most powerful symbols in witchcraft for summoning demons. Its power is sometimes explained as the intersecting of male and female "principles," with the upward-pointing triangle representing the male principle and the downward-pointing triangle the female principle.

MODERN ISRAEL AND THE HEXAGRAM

The hexagram occupies the center of the flag of the modern State of Israel. How did an occult symbol end up on the nation's flag? It comes out of an occult branch of Judaism known as Kabbalah. In the Kabbalah, it is referred to as the star of David or the shield of David, and apparently has ancient origins.

Those origins are sorcery and magic and have nothing to do with the teaching of the Bible. In fact, the mystical teachings of the Kabbalah are of a type that is repeatedly condemned by the Lord in the Bible. It seems likely that the so-called "star of David" is the star of worship denounced by the Lord in the following passage from the prophet Amos:

> "'You shall take up Sakkuth your king, and
> *Kaiwan your star-god, your images,* which you
> made for yourselves; therefore I will take you
> into exile beyond Damascus,' says the LORD,
> whose name is the God of hosts" (Amos
> 5:26–27 emphasis mine).

The image of the star-god was odious to the Lord in ancient times and still is today.

That hexagram is not a shield of the biblical King David, but a magic shield intended to ward off so-called "evil spirits." Foremost among the spirits modern Israel would keep away is the Holy Spirit of the risen Christ. The Israeli flag with its sorcerer's hexagram stands in public opposition to the message of the crucified Jesus.

Evangelical Christian preachers may be heard on the radio or TV soliciting money from Christians to send support to the State of Israel, arguing that by so doing they will "help fulfill prophecy." The prophecy they talk about fulfilling is God's promise in the Old Testament to bring his people back to their land. However, God was not meaning they would return to an earthly Israel, but rather to the kingdom of the Lord Jesus Christ.

Advertisements on *Daystar* TV say God will bless you if you send money to Israel, because you will be blessing God's people, the Jewish people. But who are God's people really? Jesus said his true mother and brothers were not those who were physically related to him, but those who heard the word of God and did it (Luke 8:21). The way to truly bless the Jews in Israel is to bring them the gospel of salvation. "Blessing" them with cash only tells them implicitly they don't need to receive the gospel.

Nature Worship

The natural world provides our food and clothing and material for homes, so Satan finds it easy to convince men to worship nature—to worship the creature rather than the Creator. God warned his people against this deception back in the time of Moses.

> "And beware lest you lift up your eyes to heaven, and when you see the sun and the moon and the stars, all the host of heaven, you be drawn away and worship them and serve them, things which the LORD your God has allotted to all the peoples under the whole heaven" (Deuteronomy 4:19).

Today we are too sophisticated to fall for this deception. Or are we? Our schools teach that everything around us—including food and clothing—comes from the big bang, not from God. The big bang determined all the laws of physics, they assert, and determined everything that has ever happened in the universe since then.

Now, most scientists would deny they worship the big bang. They would say, "It's not an object of worship; it's just something that is there." And yet, claiming that the big bang is the source of everything in the universe, including all life—

including us—is a kind of worship. When you make the big bang a substitute for God, it becomes a god itself. And scientists are offering sacrifices to this false god: The sacrifices they offer are the minds of their children and our children, who are taught in school that science is superior to the word of the true and living God. And this makes Satan the deceiver very happy.

A recent trend in the science world is the search for life on other planets. Astronomers are looking for planets which meet certain criteria which they think can support life. They say that if the conditions are right, "Life will do this," and "Life will do that," as though there is now an entity called Life with a capital L that can bring into existence individual living things all by itself. These scientists are no different than the ancients who attributed events on earth to gods like Zeus and Prometheus. When they cannot explain something, they invent a god to be the cause.

Prayers to the Dead

Another of Satan's favorite ploys over the centuries and around the world is to convince people that they can appeal to the dead for help in this life. Shinto worshipers in Japan, Hindus in India, some Indian tribes in North American, all make offerings and prayers to dead ancestors. And unfortunately the practice is present in some Christian churches. Prayers to the dead—prayers that *pretend* to be Christian prayers—can be easily found on the internet, as well as in Catholic churches. One example is the prayer to St. Anthony used by Catholics: "St. Anthony, St. Anthony please come around. Something is lost and cannot be found."

The internet has testimonies from people who maintain they prayed to St. Anthony and he found a lost object for them. The Bible tells us, however, that this kind of prayer is an abomination to God. God told the prophet Isaiah,

> "And when they say to you, 'Consult the mediums and the wizards who chirp and mutter,' should not a people consult their God? Should they consult the dead on behalf of the living?" (Isaiah 8:19).

If people consult dead spirits instead of God, it means God is not their God. There is no middle ground. God is testing us to see if we will obey him diligently.

"The LORD our God is one LORD" (Deuteronomy 6:4), and he will not give his glory to another. Séances, in which a seer attempts to bring back the spirit of a dead person and have a conversation with it, are obviously disallowed by this teaching. But so also are prayers to saints and prayers to Mary disallowed. Such prayers are prayers to false gods. They are lies. We are to pray to God in the name of Jesus Christ. Jesus died on the cross so we could do that. How can we set aside such an amazing gift which God paid for at such a terrible price? Nowhere in the Bible did God say false worship was okay if the worshiper had good intentions and pious behavior.

Sex: Yin and Yang Principles

The sex drive is powerful enough that in at least one religion it has been credited with creating the universe. That is the claim made by the Taoist religion for the so-called yin and yang principles. The yin and yang represent male and female forces, which are ostensibly so powerful as to create everything else in the universe by converging with one another. And this reminds us of a similar idea which we saw in the converging triangles of the hexagram—triangles which are said to correspond to male and female principles. We see that when Satan finds something that works on one group of people, he'll use it wherever he can on other people.

You may think, "If some people somewhere want to believe that male and female principles created the universe, let them go ahead. It's a foolish idea, but it will not affect me." But the yin and yang principles are called upon in various Eastern practices which have been imported into America, via disciplines like yoga and tai chi. And the demons being invoked are real and dangerous. American Christians have brought these practices into some churches, to display their tolerance and inclusiveness. In America the fear of being called "intolerant" often supersedes the fear of God.

One "tolerant" minister defended his church's acceptance of tai chi classes by saying in a mocking voice, "Do you mean to tell me there is something wrong with doing this?"—as he imitated one of the arm waving movements of tai chi. He was not interested in knowing that tai chi has its roots in religious beliefs which call on demons. His ministerial training had not taught him how to deal with such beliefs and probably *had* taught him that people who talked about demons were unscientific and unsophisticated.

To reply to his specific question: Sometimes arm and hand motions convey meaning. If you want me to come toward you, you can either call out, "Please come here," or you can silently use a waving motion with your hand beckoning me to come. Demons, too, understand both kinds of communication. They will respond just as well to the waving motions of tai chi as to verbal commands.

Sex: the God of Lust

To speak about demons is to invite mocking from Hollywood and from the media. The phrase "demon of lust," if it were to appear in a Hollywood movie, would most likely be spoken by a wild-eyed country preacher—a demented, killjoy character out to deprive some young couple of their right to have sex outside marriage—their right to have pleasure. Two of Satan's favorite tools are mockery and scoffing. They hide the seriousness of the truth. Yet the truth is: There is a demon of lust, and despite the scoffing—or perhaps *because* of the scoffing—this demon is one of Satan's most successful helpers.

The Bible tells us Satan tempted Eve by offering her wisdom. If she would eat of the fruit which God had forbidden, she would become wise. Today's counterpart to wisdom is pleasure. Satan says, "God knows you don't need to listen to antiquated rules about love and marriage. God knows if you disobey his rules you will only have pleasure—lots and lots of pleasure!" But when we disobey God's rules we lose control; the spirit of lust takes control of us. We become addicted to pornography. We become willing to kill our own children through abortion in order to have pleasure. We encourage our children to mutilate themselves in order to achieve some imaginary sexual identity. We open the door wide to a host of perverted "sexual identities" because the demon of lust demands its equal rights. We become slaves of lust.

The battle against sexual immorality is not a new battle. It is a battle that was fought in Bible times. The two most prominent

Canaanite objects of worship when the Israelites entered the land of Canaan were the male god Ba'al and the female goddess Ashe'rah. The two were often depicted next to one another to achieve something we have seen previously in other contexts: the convergence of male and female principles. And Ba'al and Ashe'rah were worshiped with the help of "cult prostitutes" of both sexes, meaning the demon of lust was invoked through homosexual and bisexual and lesbian activity—*as part of their religious practices.*

One place these Canaanite gods are mentioned is in the story of Gideon in the book of Judges. God called Gideon to lead a heroic military victory, but Gideon could not do so until he tore down the Canaanite shrine to Ba'al and the Ashe'rah on his father's property. Here is what the Lord commanded.

> "That night the LORD said to him, 'Take your
> father's bull, the second bull seven years old,
> and pull down the altar of Ba'al which your
> father has, and cut down the Ashe'rah that is
> beside it … '"(Judges 6:25).

Gideon could do nothing until he had gotten rid of those practices which called on the demon of lust. It is still the same with Christians today. We cannot serve God unless our house is swept clean of any pornography or anything that brings into our lives the demon of lust. That demon will keep us away from God's presence, and without God's presence we will be helpless. But today we have a great advantage over Gideon. We do not need to use a bull seven years old to pull down Ba'al's altar. Instead, we may call on the name of Jesus Christ, and in his name cast out those demons.

Triangle Power in America

The powers invoked by "triangle power" in the hexagram are being invoked by sorcerers still today. Triangle power is augmented by practitioners of magic by combining the triangles into a pyramid, giving the triangles what you might call a high-beam setting. As already pointed out, pyramid power is one of the occult powers called upon in Freemasonry—an organization common across America, and an organization whose members brim with outward respectability and may even boast that they lead church Bible studies on Sunday morning. They are very careful to keep their ceremonies secret, however, so no outsiders can see that their teachings are occult and not from Christianity at all. WICCA (witchcraft) chapters are not quite as mainline as Masonry yet, but they are not afraid to announce their presence, and they quite openly are calling on occult powers.

The existence of all these occultists in American society means demons are constantly being called upon. The people invoking demons may think they can control them, but they cannot, because the only power stronger than the demons is the power of Jesus Christ.

Analysts on the evening news and politicians and social scientists put forward many explanations for the murders and suicides and other crimes they see running rampant, and they propose laws to stop the carnage. But the fact that there is a spiritual kingdom working behind these crimes is never mentioned or thought about. The laws made by legislators never address the occult activities stirring up the demons. It is up to Christians using their prayers in the name of Jesus to come against Satan's kingdom.

Christians Without Proper Training

Christians in America today are like soldiers being sent into a battle without proper training. Our ministers are not giving the warnings and information we need about the enemy. Our watchmen do not sound the alarm and do not seem aware of what is going on in the spiritual realm—many are even embarrassed to hear talk of such things.

In Ephesians 6, Paul describes the spiritual equipment of a soldier for Christ. Paul says we are to gird ourselves with the belt of truth, the breastplate of righteousness, the shoes of the gospel of peace, the shield of faith, the helmet of salvation, and the sword of the Spirit, which is the word of God. We often hear this passage mentioned in sermons, and rightly so, because it is of fundamental importance. But then Paul adds an admonition for us to "keep alert with all perseverance" (Ephesians 6:18). Alert for what? We need knowledge of the enemy so we know what to stay alert for. We need to know the enemy's disguises to prevent him from sneaking in behind our battle lines when we aren't looking.

Deuteronomy 6:19 tells us that God's people were not instructed to waltz merrily into the promised land and receive a land that was welcoming them with open arms. Rather, they were told to enter the promised land *by thrusting out all your enemies from before you.* They were warned of the evil practices of the occupants of the land, and they were told to rid the land completely of such practices. That was their assignment then, and it is our assignment today. We are not to take on the whole armor of God only to stand around like bewildered blind men.

We are battling "against the spiritual forces of evil in the heavenly places" (Ephesians 6:12). We are battling against powers we cannot see, so we need to be aware of their stratagems. When we detect these enemies at work, we are to use our spiritual weapons to thrust them out before us. We are to do this through the power of the blood of Jesus which has already dealt Satan a mortal blow and assured us of the ultimate victory. We are to do this to give glory to God the Father, whose purpose is to use us to defeat his enemy Satan and all of Satan's demons. We are to do this because it is what we are commanded to do. We are commanded to serve as faithful and *informed* soldiers of the cross.

6
MAGIC AND SORCERY IN C.S. LEWIS

The Importance of C.S. Lewis

C.S. Lewis is often quoted in Sunday sermons and in writings by Christian authors. One could say that his status in some Protestant circles is akin to that of a saint among Roman Catholics. Lewis's books are regarded as important material for introducing children and unbelievers to the Christian faith. So if there is something wrong with those books, it is important for Christians to know about it and be warned. It is especially important for Christian parents to know that Lewis's books are the wrong way to introduce their children to Christianity because they present some harmful and ungodly teaching.

LEWIS'S BACKGROUND

Lewis did not become a Christian until he was in his thirties, at which time he was a professor of medieval literature at Oxford. He was fascinated by mythology and sorcery. The figures of ancient mythology and Arthurian legend became so vivid in his mind as to seem real. The result was that Christianity never truly superseded mythology in Lewis's mind. Christianity landed on top of the pile, but it never removed the pile.

Mythology Does Not Mix with Christianity

The books in Lewis's *Chronicles of Narnia* series portray ordinary human children encountering centaurs, unicorns, fauns, satyrs, and dryads (Lewis describes one dryad as "a nymph of a beech tree," *The Last Battle*, 21). But Lewis is not trying to give us a lesson about Greek mythology, showing us how silly Greek religious thinking was. His story is intended to illustrate elements of Christian theology for children. In the Bible, however, creatures like these are condemned as Satanic elements of pagan religions. Satyrs, for example, were objects of worship which drew the people of Israel away from God. God instructed Moses to warn the people away from such worship, saying, "So they shall no more slay their sacrifices for satyrs, after whom they play the harlot" (Leviticus 17:7). In the Bible, such creatures appear only in desolate places where God is absent. For example, in this passage in Isaiah, God is describing what Edom will look like when God takes vengeance on her: "And wild beasts shall meet with hyenas, the satyr shall cry to his fellow; yea, there shall the night hag alight, and find for herself a resting place" (Isaiah 34:14). Yet in Lewis's literary universe, such creatures appear as morally neutral—sometimes on God's side and sometimes on the enemy's side.

Lewis's knowledge of such creatures is far ranging. He brings in Jinns—demon spirits from Arab tradition which are mentioned in the Qur'an. And he speaks of Lilith—the supposed "first wife" of Adam—as though her existence were historical fact, rather than an invention of Jewish mythology (*The Lion, the Witch and the Wardrobe*, 88). When Lewis runs out of strange beings in the spiritual world, he doesn't hesitate to invent new ones, as with his "eldils" in *That Hideous Strength*.

Magic Does Not Mix with Christianity

Most crucially, nothing important happens in Lewis's fiction without magic being involved. (Here we are not talking about sleight-of-hand magic, we're talking about real magic which calls on demonic powers of the air.) The children in *The Lion, the Witch and the Wardrobe* are transported from one world to another by magic. In fact, magic is honored with a capital M, "Magic" (e.g. in *The Last Battle*, 158). In the *Chronicles of Narnia* series, Aslan the lion represents a Christ figure, and even this Christ figure appears to depend on magic, as when he brings a "magic spring" to melt away the witch's winter (*The Lion, the Witch and the Wardrobe*, 136).

In the Bible, it would be anathema to describe Jesus or any of God's prophets as performing miracles by use of magic. Included in the law that Moses gave to the people of Israel was the following commandment:

> "There shall not be found among you any
> one who burns his son or his daughter as an
> offering, anyone who practices divination,
> a soothsayer, or an augur, or a sorcerer, or
> a charmer, or a medium, or a wizard, or a
> necromancer. For whoever does these things is
> an abomination to the LORD; and because of
> these abominable practices the LORD your God
> is driving them out before you. You shall be

blameless before the LORD your God. For these nations, which you are about to dispossess, give heed to soothsayers and to diviners; but as for you, the LORD your God has not allowed you so to do" (Deuteronomy 18:10–14).

In the New Testament, we read how the Apostles continually preached against those who practiced magic arts. One result is recorded in the book of Acts:

"Many also of those who were now believers came, confessing and divulging their practices. And a number of those who practiced magic arts brought their books together and burned them in the sight of all; and they counted the value of them and found it came to fifty thousand pieces of silver. So the word of the Lord grew and prevailed mightily" (Acts 19:18–20).

The word of the Lord grew and prevailed mightily—*against the world of sorcery and magic,* that is.

MERLIN THE MAGICIAN CANNOT BE A CHRISTIAN, AS LEWIS CLAIMS

In *That Hideous Strength*, Lewis does something extraordinary: He has Merlin the magician *resurrected* from his sixth century grave into modern England. This resurrection is accomplished with no mention of God or Christ, as though self-resurrection is something one could expect from a powerful magician. Lewis has Dr. Dimble explain Merlin's role when he wonders "whether Merlin doesn't represent the last trace of something the later tradition has quite forgotten about—something that became impossible when the only people in touch with the supernatural were either white or black, either priests or sorcerers" (*That Hideous Strength*, 30). Which is to say, Lewis entertains the thought that magic is not necessarily evil: maybe there is some in-between area. Later in the book, Ransom thinks "Merlin's art was the last survival of something ... going back to an era in which the general relations of mind and matter on this planet had been other than those we know" (p. 198). Still later, Ransom (who is the authoritative figure for those supposedly on the side of God) declares Merlin to be a Christian (p. 277). In simple terms, Merlin represents in Lewis's world a re-birth of what might be called "good magic"—a thing the Bible unequivocally declares to be impossible. And Lewis even portrays this magic as compatible with Christianity.

By the way, the resurrected Merlin remains a magician after his resurrection in Lewis's story. He is identified as a druid (p. 283), he can hypnotize people at will (p. 327), and he can make a tramp speak a foreign language (p. 331), just to cite a few examples. These are signs that Merlin is invoking demonic powers, even though Lewis portrays Merlin's actions as happening toward a good end, and as the actions of a Christian.

Clairvoyance is Condemned by God

In *That Hideous Strength*, there is also a character named Jane who is referred to as a "seer." Jane has dreams which foretell future events. In other words, Jane is a clairvoyant—a person with psychic powers that are not from God. In the book, this ability is termed a "faculty" of Jane's which she has inherited (p. 236) and which is not dependent on any relationship with God (Jane is not a Christian).

Jane's powers to foresee the future through dreams are to be contrasted with the powers of Joseph in the Bible. When Pharaoh told Joseph he had heard that Joseph could interpret dreams, Joseph replied: "*It is not in me*; God will give Pharaoh a favorable answer" (Genesis 41:16 emphasis mine). The biblical prophet Daniel also interpreted dreams, and he made a similar statement before interpreting King Nebuchadnezzar's dream.

> "Daniel answered the king, '*No wise men, enchanters, magicians, or astrologers can show to the king the mystery which the king has asked*, but there is a God in heaven who reveals mysteries, and he has made known to King Nebuchadnezzar what will be in the latter days'" (Daniel 2:27–28 emphasis mine).

Both Daniel and Joseph went out of their way to make it clear they had no special powers beyond those of any other human being. Their interpretations of dreams came from God, not from some faculty inherent in them.

Lewis makes it appear that in his world magic powers and sorcery can be used to good ends, and in some cases, they can accomplish things which (according to the Bible) can only be accomplished by God Almighty. Lewis is giving glory to demonic powers for things that can only come from God.

Astrology Does Not Mix with Christianity

As *That Hideous Strength* progresses, we find Merlin acknowledging that Dr. Ransom has even greater powers than Merlin, and Merlin gives worship to Ransom. At this point Ransom is seen as a Christ figure, because Ransom is the leader of those who use supernatural powers to defeat the evil N.I.C.E. organization. (The N.I.C.E. organization evidently is intended to serve as a parody of the Nazi party in World War II.) Then we read this astonishing statement by Dr. Ransom: "I have stood before Mars himself in the sphere of Mars and before Venus herself in the sphere of Venus. It is their strength, and the strength of some greater than they, which will destroy our enemies" (p. 287). Lewis's spiritual train has come completely off the track. He has a Christ figure declaring that astrology has hidden, saving powers to destroy evil, whereas we know from the Bible that astrology is a tool of Satan.

Platonic Philosophy Does Not Mix with Christianity

The world of sorcery does not provide sufficient false teaching to satisfy Lewis; he also brings in Platonic philosophy. In *The Last Battle* (p. 195), Lord Digory tells the children that the Narnia they lived in "was not the real Narnia. That had a beginning and an end. It was only a shadow or a copy of the real Narnia which has always been here and always will be here: just as our own world, England and all, is only a shadow or copy of something in Aslan's real world." Then he adds: "It's all in Plato, all in Plato: bless me, what *do* they teach them at these schools!"

Lord Digory is referring to the Platonic analogy in which Plato imagines himself sitting near a campfire inside a cave. When he turns his back to the fire, he is staring at the wall of the cave, and he notices that any objects which are between the wall of the cave and the fire will cast shadows onto the wall. He cannot see the objects themselves from where he is sitting, but he can see their shadows on the cave wall. He likens those shadows to our present world, and he sees the objects which are casting the shadows as the real or original world. So Lewis is suggesting what the Christians call heaven is equivalent to Plato's "real" world, and our present world is equivalent to Plato's shadows on the wall.

But this teaching of Plato is not at all biblical. The Bible says after this world is gone there will be a *new* heaven and a *new* earth which God "will" create (future tense, see Isaiah 66:22 and 2 Peter 3:13 for example). According to the Bible, this present world is not a shadow of something which already exists in heaven—some original or ideal world. This world we live in is a completely real and completely original creation of God. It is not a projection of some other, more *real* world. In fact, the Bible suggests that the new earth we inherit after this life will be a perfect version of this earth—a version without evil, and filled with God's love. In other words, the Bible reverses Plato's order of things. *This* earth comes first, and then the new, perfect earth comes later.

The Wisdom of this World is Folly with God

"For the wisdom of this world is folly with God" (1 Corinthians 3:19).

In the end, Lewis provides us with an example in his own person of how the wisdom of this world can corrupt our thinking. Lewis's mind was so filled with worldly wisdom that he was unable to shake loose from all his learning and approach the Bible on its own terms. He was unable to see the Bible as a document containing wisdom which supersedes all other wisdom.

Parents, teach your children the Bible—*from the Bible itself*—not from C.S. Lewis. College students, if you try to reconcile C.S. Lewis's fantasies with the teachings of the Bible, you will only end up in a muddle. The wisdom of the Bible (which is the wisdom of God) does not mix with any philosophy or any other religion in the world. It stands on its own and supersedes all others. New believers, if you want to learn about Christianity, pick up a Bible and begin by reading the gospel of Matthew. Don't try to figure it out from C.S. Lewis. Do not try to understand the Lord Jesus Christ from reading about Aslan the lion or about Dr. Ransom who led the victory over N.I.C.E.

God's word is nothing like the words of the philosophers, or the stories of Greek mythology, or the tales of medieval literature, or the fantasies of C.S. Lewis. "Is not my word like fire, says the LORD, and like a hammer which breaks the rock in pieces?" (Jeremiah 23:29).

7
BLACK LIVES MATTER

The Deceptions of Black Lives Matter

Forces which hate Christians in America are moving in at lightning speed. Satan is hard at work using lies and deception to keep Christians off balance. One outstanding example of those deceptions is the Black Lives Matter (BLM) movement.

Christians (*especially black Christians*) need to know that below the surface, the Black Lives Matter movement is not "black." BLM was founded by black women, but they were in turn trained by a white man named Eric Mann, a Communist whose recommended reading list (the list he uses for training) is topped by writings of Karl Marx, Frederick Engels, W.E.B DuBois, and V.I. Lenin. Marx, Engels, and Lenin are white men, and DuBois is of mixed black and European descent. The writings of these men present the basics of the Communist creed. They present sophisticated arguments for organizing a society based on materialism—on the belief that everything in the universe (including all people both black and white) is nothing more than an arrangement of molecules. There is no God in charge. Religion is the "opiate of the people," as Marx famously said. Blacks and whites alike are of no ultimate value, because they are reduced to masses of molecules.

Christians also need to know that Black Lives Matter is not about "lives," except in the sense that lives are quite expendable in the service of the BLM cause. This expendability comes as a logical consequence of materialism. Since there is no soul and no spirit—only a mass of molecules—life is devalued. Life is a concept we have invented to help us communicate about what we see around us. The claim made in the Bible about Jesus, that "in him was life, and the life was the light of men" (John 1:4), is rendered meaningless.

Christianity is the Avowed Enemy

The low value placed on life by Communism should be apparent from the millions of lives (by most counts, *hundreds* of millions) sacrificed in Communist purges in Russia, China, Vietnam, Cambodia, North Korea, and elsewhere. Chief among the targets in all these purges have been Christians. And it is already clear that the chief target of the purge planned for America is Christianity and its promise of eternal life.

The violent methods used in Communist revolutions in those other countries are now being used in America. Rational argument is thrown aside in favor of Molotov cocktails, bricks, smashed windows, looted stores, and burned vehicles. Black Christians need to know that they will be no better off than other Christians under this revolution. The true target of BLM and the organization's Communist masters is not racism, it is not white oppressors—it is Christianity.

SCHOOLS HAVE PREPARED OUR YOUTH

America's young people have been well-prepared for the revolution by Satan's proxies working in our schools. Youth have been taught scientific materialism, and taught to dismiss the Bible as unscientific myth. They have been taught to adhere to the LGBTQ platform of inclusiveness by giving honor to sexual depravity. Students have been taught to reject the Christian idea of a family as consisting of husband and wife and children, and to replace it with whatever grouping strikes one's fancy. *The rejection of the nuclear family and promotions of LGBTQ interests are all important parts of the BLM platform, as stated clearly on their website.*

WHY THE REJECTION OF CHRISTIANITY IS IMPORTANT TO BLM

The Christian views himself as standing before the judgment seat of God first and man second. To Communists this idea represents a challenge to the authority of the state, and must be suppressed. In America, answerability to God has been the moral strength of a nation. In America, Christianity has historically meant that when enough of its citizens are guided by Christian ethical standards, then the state has not needed to be the sole enforcer of various kinds of morality (do not steal, do not murder, do not commit adultery, etc.). The Christian's conscience and the Christian community would enforce these laws. Christianity historically has allowed Americans to preserve their freedom because the state did not have to step in to dictate moral order in every person's life. And the so-called Protestant work ethic has meant that people followed the Apostle Paul's admonition to work with their hands, and if anyone did not work for himself he would not eat.

Why the Violent Attacks on Small Businesses?

The violent mobs inspired by the BLM movement are attacking small businesses and police headquarters. In some cases, the small businesses are owned by blacks, and in some cases the police are blacks. In other words, BLM attacks blacks as well as whites. But these facts are of no consequence to the organizers. What matters is that small businesses represent traditional, pull-yourself-up-by-the-bootstraps American freedom and initiative. And the police are the ones protecting the freedom of these businesses. Small businesses represent an opportunity for Americans to thrive without swearing allegiance to the diversity/tolerance code of the LGBTQ people. Small businesses represent the opportunity for Americans to prosper while practicing Christianity "under the radar" of the political correctness police. Therefore, small businesses must go.

Big business is already firmly under the control of the LGBTQ, anti-Christian thought police. Every employee in big business in America must undergo "diversity training" and show allegiance to LGBTQ thinking to stay employed. Companies like Google and Facebook are not besieged by angry BLM mobs. In fact, news reports tell us that big tech companies send money to BLM to help promote the revolution. (More about thought police in a later chapter.)

The Result that is Planned
for Us

Communist documents do not preach change through existing political institutions. They preach change through "conflict"—which means violent revolution and a complete sweeping away of the existing system of government. The Communist Party (or its substitute by a different name) must control all "means of production," with no private ownership of business. They preach atheism, which means they either shut down all places of worship, or they leave a few representative places of worship open so they can pretend to the world that they support human rights. (They will, however, install puppet priests and send spies to such places of worship to maintain thought control.)

Without Christianity, without police, and with the fomenting of rebellion, there will be uncontrolled violence. (We are already seeing it.) One out-of-control group will incite other groups to reply. People will not object when a totalitarian power steps in to preserve order, to make the streets safe to walk again. They will allow the Communist Party or its woke equivalent to take control and suppress dissent. That is the plan.

THE REAL GOAL

What is the Communist (and BLM) motivation for such drastic and violent action? Communists say they are fighting against economic injustice between social classes, and class warfare is necessary to right the injustice. But in the specific case of BLM, the claim is made that the injustice is to a race. The problem, they say, is the injustice to black Americans by white Americans.

The difference between class and race is of great importance to American blacks. The Communist creed—which is the heart of the BLM creed—says the middle class of a nation must be sacrificed to the cause of economic justice and their assets transferred to the poor "working class." The BLM may say they stand for blacks against whites, but their Communist ideology is directed against all middle-class people, regardless of race. According to one study available on the internet (statista.com/statistics/500290/share-of-us-middle-class-by-race-and-ethnicity), as of 2015, 45% of blacks were middle class, as compared with a very similar 52% of whites. When the Communist BLM regime takes control and the redistribution of wealth begins, black assets stand to be looted at almost the same rate as whites.

Those statistics summarize prospects for the economic situation. As for the religious situation, all Christians, whether black or white, will see that the ultimate motivation of BLM is to serve Satan and rid America of the bothersome Christian morality which still raises its head now and then. If the name of Jesus is only heard as a curse word, Satan will be delighted.

8
CHURCH MUSIC: WHAT IN THE WORLD IS GOING ON?

It's Not Just the Loud Volume

As the years progress for this writer, loud noises no longer seem merely unpleasant, they've become downright painful. The standard setup nowadays features electric guitars, electric keyboards, rock-band-size drum sets, and high-wattage amplifiers with the volume knob turned far to the right. Psalm 150 said to praise God "with loud clashing cymbals," but that was outdoors with no electronic amplification. Many church services today are so loud that people like me have no choice but to get up and leave. We are excluded from worship.

Besides the volume, there are two other disturbing elements in modern church music. Many churches have replaced hymns with so-called choruses—snippets of music that repeat the same words to the point of monotony. And another element, which serves to augment the effect of the repetitious words, is a steady, hard-driving beat.

Why should these things be a problem, you may ask, if the words are words of praise? Maybe it is a musical style I don't like, while other people like it. Just because I don't like it, does that mean there's something wrong with it?

In response, recall how a magician can hypnotize a subject by dangling a swinging, glittering pendulum before the subject's eyes. There is a musical equivalent to that magician's pendulum. A driving beat, combined with words and melodic snatches which repeat, can have a hypnotic effect. They can cast a spell. And what is a "spell" exactly? A spell happens when one's mind becomes open and passive so that demonic powers can enter and take control—not something we want to happen in church!

The Appeal to Young People

So why are churches allowing this? You have probably heard the same explanation I have heard, and maybe you have repeated it yourself: "This music attracts young people. Even if they come for the music, at least then they will stay and hear a sermon preached." And young people (and older people who like the music) may say, "The music makes me feel closer to God." And my reply would be, "Are you sure it is God you are getting closer to?"

A SIGN OF GOD'S PRESENCE?

Christianity inherits an amazing heritage of beautiful music—music of true and lasting beauty, written by great composers and poets over hundreds of years. Our God is the creator of all things beautiful, especially the creator of beautiful music. This modern loud, thumping, hypnotic music is not beautiful. If young people today are rejecting their heritage of beautiful music, maybe that is a sign—a sign not of God's presence, but a sign that music in worship services has become a distraction.

The John the Baptist Challenge

Here is a challenge to our churches: Remove the distraction, even in churches that present only traditional music. Maybe it is time to remove music entirely from worship services and see who will show up simply to hear the preaching of the Word. Maybe it is time to think about the crowds that walked miles out into the wilderness to hear John the Baptist preach. They went to a place that had no McDonalds and no taxi service—and certainly no drums and electric guitars. And what did they hear when they got there? They were not given lectures on inclusiveness and tolerance and a "warm welcome to all." Quite the opposite. They were told that they were sinners and they must "repent, for the kingdom of heaven is at hand." When the Pharisees and Sadducees came to John, they were met with this jolly greeting:

> "You brood of vipers! Who warned you to flee from the wrath to come? Bear fruit that befits repentance, and do not presume to say to yourselves, 'We have Abraham as our father'; for I tell you, God is able from these stones to raise up children to Abraham. Even now the axe is laid to the root of the trees; every tree therefore that does not bear good fruit is cut down and thrown into the fire" (Matthew 3:7-10).

Preaching like that, combined with no music and no coffee and doughnuts after the service, is not the way to build a mega-church.

GIVE YOUR CHURCH A COMPLACENCY TEST

Here is a complacency test for your church: Get rid of the music and see what is left. Get rid of drums, guitars, and keyboards. Let the organ and piano be silent, too. Ask God to replace the power of the amplifiers with the power of the Holy Spirit.

Get rid of the music, then see who shows up. See who hungers enough for the word of God that they will show up, even when there is no entertainment.

Remove the music and see who will come for washing away of sin.

Remove the drums and guitars and see who will come for healing.

Remove the coffee and doughnuts and see who will come for God's Word.

When you see these people, know they are the ones who will survive the times that are ahead.

9
ISLAM AND CHRISTIANITY

The Shock of 9/11

9/11 came as a shock to America, but most Americans have been reluctant to understand the meaning of the shock. The American spirit wants to believe all people can be our friends if we just get to know them ("I never met a man I didn't like," as Will Rogers said), and so we shouldn't let a few oddball terrorists upset our thinking.

America historically has been shielded from most of the world by two oceans. The shield is not just physical, but emotional and psychological. We don't give much thought to a man living somewhere on the edge of the Sahara Desert, so why should he think about us? We don't give much thought to a family living in a teeming city in Pakistan, so why should they think about us? But they do think about us. To them America is thought of as a Christian country, and the Muslim religion which they practice diligently every day tells them Christianity is the enemy—Christians are to be oppressed and suppressed by any means possible. America to many of them is "the great Satan."

Christians Hear What They Want to Hear

A preacher in my hometown distributed fliers in mailboxes saying he was going to talk about Islam on Sunday. I thought he was going to issue a warning that Christianity was under attack, so I went to hear what he had to say.

Instead of issuing a warning, he raised a white flag of surrender. The minister gave some innocuous biographical facts about Muhammad, admitted that he had just spent a couple of hours leafing through the Qur'an (the holy book of Islam), and concluded that the Qur'an seemed a lot like our Old Testament. Then he recounted some positive social interactions he had had with Muslims in our town, said they were certainly nice people and therefore we should be nice to them. And the congregation gave him a standing ovation. They applauded him for his "loving" inclusiveness. They applauded him because instead of warning them, he was giving them a heavy dose of warm, fuzzy American tolerance.

American Christians don't want to say bad things about other people. It doesn't seem "Christian." It seems uncharitable. But assessing a religion based on whether a few of its adherents are nice to you is intellectually dishonest.

Most Christians who follow the news have probably thought of some of the questions about Islam which I list below. None of these questions was asked—let alone answered—in the sermon I heard. The answers show Islam to be the opposite of warm and fuzzy and tolerant.

Question 1:
Do Muslims and Christians Worship the Same God?

The short answer is: No.

This answer could be especially confusing in some predominantly Muslim countries, because in their language Christians and Muslims usually end up using the same word for God—"Allah." There is no specifically Christian word for God in those languages. Looking back in history, some Jewish and Christian Arabs used the word "Allah" for God long before the time of Muhammad, and Muhammad adopted the word for God already in use by Jews and Christians.

Since the word for God is the same, is he the same? Absolutely not. *Adherents of the two religions worship two completely different Gods.* That can be seen most clearly by comparing the Muslim view of Jesus, as revealed in the Qur'an, versus the Christian view. We will highlight those differences; but first, a bit of history.

THE ORIGINS OF ISLAM

Muslims trace their religious beliefs to three sources: the life of Muhammad (the founder of Islam), the sayings attributed to Muhammad (called hadith), and the Qur'an (Islam's sacred book). Of these three sources, the Qur'an is considered the most important and most authoritative, so I will focus mainly on the Qur'an.

The Qur'an was written by one man—Muhammad (A.D. 570–632)—over a span of 23 years. The Bible, by contrast, was penned by 40 different authors over a period of about 1600 years. The Qur'an is about one third the size of the Bible, and is dependent on the Bible for much of its subject matter. The Qur'an singles out some of the most prominent people in the Bible—Abraham, Moses, and Jesus—and proposes to correct what the Bible says about them. Even though the Bible documents itself exhaustively with thousands of names, genealogies, dates, places, and eyewitness testimonies (none of which can be found in the Qur'an), Muslims believe our Bible has been corrupted and the Qur'an gives the correct interpretation. This is what the imams (Muslim preachers) tell their congregations.

The Qur'an was given to Muhammad during trances when a spirit spoke to him. The first time Muhammad experienced one of these trances, he recoiled from it and thought he had been visited by demons. But eventually his wife convinced him he was being visited by Allah, and so he continued to await these visions and record what he was told. (My opinion is Muhammad was right the first time.)

The first part of Muhammad's life was spent as a prosperous businessman, overseeing the caravan trading business of the woman who would become his first wife (she was fifteen years older than he). The second part of Muhammad's life was spent as a military leader, fighting to spread his religious beliefs throughout Arabia. As a military leader, he was known for being sometimes generous, sometimes brutal and ruthless. The Qur'an was written in a time that spanned both periods of Muhammad's life. Muslim theologians have declared that whenever there are contradictions in the Qur'an, the passages written during the later militant (and brutal) period will override the passages written during the earlier peaceful period. Which means, if you hear someone quote the Qur'an with a message about peace, they are probably not giving you the whole picture.

THE MUSLIM VIEW OF JESUS

The Qur'an speaks extensively about Jesus, and Muslims believe that Jesus was a real person. However, they consider him to be a prophet, not the Savior. They believe that Jesus was not the Son of God, that Jesus did not die on the cross, and therefore that Jesus was not resurrected from the dead. They do not believe that Jesus took our sins upon himself and become our Savior.

The demon spirit that spoke to Muhammad told him it was blasphemy "to associate" any person with God, and it was blasphemy to say that God would have a Son (Jesus). The spirit accused Christians of worshiping God and Jesus and Mary, all three, hence Christians (the demon spirit concluded) were really polytheists, whereas Islam was the religion of true monotheism—the worship of one God. The spirit that spoke to Muhammad claimed Allah would never allow a prophet of his to die a disgraceful death on a cross, so that assumption is the basis for Islam's claim that the crucifixion never happened. And for Muhammad that meant Jesus never died for our sins.

Some people might hear these things and conclude that Muslims simply have different beliefs about Jesus than we do, and leave it at that, as though to say, "Okay, next topic." But the subject of Jesus is not a topic to be dismissed so easily. Jesus is the most important topic there could be. The Apostle John made the following statements in his first epistle.

> "Who is the liar but he who denies that Jesus is the Christ? This is the antichrist, he who denies the Father and the Son" (1 John 2:22).

"Every spirit which does not confess Jesus is not of God. This is the spirit of antichrist, of which you heard that it was coming, and now it is in the world already" (1 John 4:3).

Now, if you go around speaking about "the spirit of antichrist" in public (or even in some churches), many people will dismiss you as a Bible-thumping, fundamentalist kook. But the Apostle John was definitely not a kook. John was given great spiritual insight by the Holy Spirit, and he was given the responsibility of transferring that insight to us—the responsibility of warning us (which he did through the books of the Bible bearing his name, and the book of Revelation).

So what is the implication for Islam and its holy book, the Qur'an? Islam is the only major religion to arise after the time of Christ, and so *Islam is the only religion with a holy book that specifically, and by name, denies that Jesus is the Christ.* When you read the words of John ("Who is the liar but he who denies that Jesus is the Christ?") it is almost as though he was anticipating the words of the Qur'an. *According to John, it is perfectly clear that the voice speaking to Muhammad was a lying spirit, a spirit sent by the father of lies, Satan.* Remember the words Jesus spoke to the Jews who were opposing him—words that also apply to Muhammad. Jesus said, "You are of your father the devil, and your will is to do your father's desires.... When he lies, he speaks according to his own nature, for he is a liar and the father of lies" (John 8:44).

Islam does not simply have a different view of Jesus. Islam has a Satanic view of Jesus. And since Satan is the source of the writings in the Qur'an that pertain to Jesus, Satan must then be the source of the entire Qur'an. Christians need to be warned that though their Muslim neighbors may be friendly, and though they are "people just like us," they are the victims of a teaching that is Satanic in origin. (We will talk later about a Christian response to Muslims.)

The Allah of the Qur'an is Not a God of Love

A Christian who is reading the Qur'an for the first time may gradually sense that there is something missing, and then it suddenly strikes home. The word "love" is almost completely absent from the Qur'an. The whole tone of the Qur'an is one of threats. In effect, Allah says throughout the Qur'an, "You better believe in me, and you better do as I say... *or else.*"

Allah is not a god of love, as is the God of the Bible. The few times love is mentioned in the Qur'an, it has a different meaning than love has in the Bible. Chapter 3 of the Qur'an says that "Allah loves those who act aright," but "Allah does not love those who do wrong" (Qur'an 3:76, 57). Allah loves you only when you meet his requirements. The Bible says "God *is* love" (1 John 4:16 emphasis mine). Love is the essence of the God of the Bible. Love defines who God is. God cannot love any more or any less depending on our actions. God's love for us is so great that it is beyond our comprehension, regardless of what we may say or do.

A Muslim woman named Wafa Sultan wrote a book about her experiences growing up in a Muslim society in Syria, and titled her book *A God Who Hates.* That is her description of the Allah of the Qur'an. What a contrast to the God of the Bible, who throughout both the Old and New Testaments is described as a God of love. In the Old Testament, the Hebrew word "hesed," translated as "steadfast love," applies to God— meaning God's love is never dimmed. God's love is eternal. And in the New Testament, God makes the ultimate sacrifice of love by offering his only Son on the cross, to enable us to enter his kingdom and spend eternity with him.

The Qur'an, on the other hand, not only almost completely avoids the word love, but specifically denies that Jesus' sacrifice on the cross ever happened. The greatest act of love in the history of the universe—the sacrifice of Jesus on the cross for our sins—is said by the Qur'an to be counter to the nature of Allah.

According to the Qur'an, it is blasphemy to say that God has a son, and it is blasphemy to say that God would even allow one of his prophets to die on a cross. (The Qur'an says that Jesus was a prophet but not the Son of God.) Christians worship the God of the Bible specifically because he is the God and Father of our Lord Jesus Christ, without whose sacrifice we would have no salvation. The Allah of Islam is not a father, and he has no son who died for our salvation. Whatever love he may exhibit is purely conditional. We conclude that the God of the Bible is *not* the god of Islam, and the Allah of Islam is *not* the God of the Bible.

Before leaving this subject, let's review some verses in John's first epistle.

> "In this is love, not that we loved God but that he loved us and sent his Son to be the expiation for our sins" (1 John 4:10).

> "So we know and believe the love God has for us. God is love, and he who abides in love abides in God, and God abides in him" (1 John 4:16).

If you read through the entire Qur'an, you will come back to the Bible and read the first epistle of John with a deep sigh of relief. Feelings of oppression will be lifted, and your gratitude for the Bible's message of grace will be greatly increased.

If this seems like an unfriendly characterization of the Qur'an, then it should be noted that the Qur'an has many—in fact, very many—disparaging and hostile things to say about Christians and Jews (often grouped together as "People of the Book," where the word "Book" is a reference to our Bible), and about the Christian religion. For example, Qur'an 98:6 calls People of the Book "the worst of creatures," according to some translations—even "vilest of creatures" in other translations. Unfriendly would be a great understatement of the Qur'an's view of Christians.

Question 2:
Can a Muslim be
President?

You may recall when 2016 presidential candidate Dr. Ben Carson was asked this question, he caused a furor by replying that no, a Muslim could not be President. The furor came from indignant Americans saying, "Our Constitution guarantees freedom of religion, and freedom of religion applies to politicians just as much as it applies to anyone else."

Of course, on a very simplistic level, if a majority of citizens voted for a Muslim to be President, then he would become president. But here's the problem: Islam is not just a religion; it is also a political system. Islam includes not just a theology, but a legal system called Sharia law. Sharia law and the U.S. Constitution are completely incompatible. If a Muslim were to become President, where would his deepest loyalty be—to the U.S. Constitution or to Sharia law? If a Muslim were to become President, and if he were true to his Muslim religion, he would be obliged to do everything in his power to replace the U.S. Constitution with Sharia law. Sharia law would dictate that the U.S. be run by Muslim clerics, and at the head of those clerics would be a caliph—perhaps even the caliph proclaimed by a terrorist group like ISIS. There would be no more Bill of Rights. There would be only the laws dictated by a ruthless seventh-century warlord. (Why are American media and political leaders—*and Christian leaders*—so ignorant of these facts? It's all there, written in black and white for everyone to read.)

Question 3:
Are Terrorist Groups like Isis and Al-Qaeda Truly Muslim, or is Islam a Religion of Peace?

You have probably heard the claim that Islam is a religion of peace, and terrorists are not truly Muslim. That is what many government leaders and journalists have tried to tell us, sticking their heads firmly in the ground like ostriches. But the jihadis (Muslim terrorists) in these different terrorist groups quote the Qur'an and proclaim loudly they are fighting in the name of Allah.

Are the terrorists' claims justified by Muslim scripture? Yes, they are, absolutely. When you read the Qur'an, you will see it is a book written by a seventh-century warlord commanding his followers to behave, well ... like seventh-century warlords.

The militant life of Muhammad is a dramatic contrast to the life of Jesus. And Muhammad has left clear instructions in the Qur'an for his followers to act just as he did. Here are two examples from the Qur'an:

Qur'an chapter 9:5 says, "fight and slay the Pagans [any non-Muslims] wherever you find them, and seize them, beleaguer them, and lie in wait for them in every stratagem (of war)."

Qur'an 9:29 says: "Fight those who do not believe in Allah or the Last Day ... nor acknowledge the Religion of Truth [Islam], (even if they are of) the People of the Book [Christians and Jews]."

ATTAINING MUSLIM PARADISE

Muslim teaching says to do your best to obey all of Allah's rules, and at his discretion he will allow you into Paradise after this life. Gaining admission to Paradise is portrayed as an iffy proposition, and Allah is seen to be quixotic and unpredictable in his decisions. There is one and only one act that can give a Muslim an absolute guarantee of entering Paradise after death, and that is to die in jihad (warfare against unbelievers). Qur'an 9:111 says, "Allah has purchased of the Believers [Muslims] their persons and their goods; for theirs (in return) is the Garden (of Paradise): they fight in His Cause, and slay and are slain: a promise binding on him in Truth, through the Law, the Gospel, and the Qur'an: and who is more faithful to his covenant than Allah? *Then rejoice in the bargain which you have concluded: that is the supreme achievement.*" I have added italics to the sentence that must especially catch the attention of young jihadis. That sentence gives them a suicide bargain with Allah. It tells them if they die in some act of jihad (warfare against unbelievers), they are guaranteed entry to Paradise. And notice something else that seems almost unbelievable: The Qur'an is claiming the authority of the Law (the Old Testament) and the Gospel (the New Testament) in establishing jihad against Christians and Jews!

THE MORAL CODE OF ISLAM

What about the moral code (or lack thereof) of the terrorist groups? Can that be in any way associated with Islam? Many of their practices that seem barbaric to us are encoded in Sharia law. Following are some examples with supporting citations from the Qur'an.

> Sharia law authorizes slavery, in particular, sex slavery (see Qur'an 23:6, 4:3, 4:24).

Sharia law authorizes sex trafficking (see Qur'an 8:41).

Sharia law authorizes a Muslim man to have as many as four wives, plus unlimited sex slaves (see Qur'an 4:3). (But note that Muhammad himself—who is supposed to serve as a model for other Muslims—broke his own rule and had eleven wives and two concubines. One of his wives had been his daughter-in-law, and another wife was only nine years old when the marriage was consummated. Muhammad, who is supposed to stand as an example for all Muslims, was guilty of both hypocrisy and sexual immorality.)

Sharia law authorizes wife beating (see Qur'an 4:34).

Sharia law authorizes Draconian punishments like cutting off hands and legs of thieves, and whipping women who show a bit too much skin in public (see Qur'an 5:33–34, 38).

The Qur'an exhorts Muslims to fight, terrify, demean, and kill unbelievers, with Christians specifically singled out as unbelievers (see Qur'an 2:193, 4:89, 5:51, 8:13–17, 8:59–60, 9:29).

Seeing the above examples makes one wonder how many Muslims have actually read the Qur'an. Surely some would say to themselves, "This is nasty stuff! Why am I basing my life on this book?"

A BIBLICAL PROPHECY ABOUT ISLAM

According to the book of Genesis, Abraham had two sons. One was named Ishmael, who was born to an Egyptian slave woman named Hagar. The other was named Isaac, who was born to Abraham's wife, Sarah. Christians and Jews trace their religious heritage back to Isaac. Muslims trace their religion back to Ishmael and claim that God's blessing was upon Ishmael rather than upon Isaac (reversing the Bible's version).

I mention this because the Bible contains a revealing prophecy about Ishmael, whom Muslims claim as their ancestor. Before Ishmael was born, the Lord spoke this prophecy to Ishmael's mother Hagar.

> "He [Ishmael] shall be a wild ass of a man, his hand against every man and every man's hand against him; and he shall dwell over against all his kinsmen" (Genesis 16:12).

Isn't that a perfect description of the world of Islam today—their hands "against every man" (even other Muslims), and "every man's hand against" them? God foresaw the conflict Ishmael and his descendants would bring to earth.

How to Defeat a Religion of Fear

Islam is a religion of fear, and the Islamic militants hope to afflict us with a spirit of fear. Even in places in America where they cannot bring their guns, they know they can still afflict us if they can instill fear in our hearts. Fear is as much our enemy as guns and bombs.

RECEIVE THE PEACE OF CHRIST

The word of God equips us to fight against fear. When Jesus knew the time of his crucifixion was near, he knew the Enemy would assault his disciples with fear and doubts. So he gave them this assurance.

> "Peace I leave with you; my peace I give to you; not as the world gives do I give to you. Let not your hearts be troubled, neither let them be afraid" (John 14:27).

And when Paul wanted to encourage the Philippians to continue in the faith and not fall away, he told them:

> "Have no anxiety about anything, but in everything by prayer and supplication with

thanksgiving let your requests be made known to God. And the peace of God, which passes all understanding, will keep your hearts and your minds in Christ Jesus" (Philippians 4:6–7).

Paul was in a Roman prison at the time he wrote those words, facing possible execution, and yet he persevered in seeking God's peace. He gave the Philippians yet another insight.

"Finally, brethren, whatever is true, whatever is honorable, whatever is just, whatever is pure, whatever is lovely, whatever is gracious, if there is any excellence, if there is anything worthy of praise, think about these things. What you have learned and received and heard and seen in me, do; and *the God of peace will be with you*" (Philippians 4:8–9 emphasis mine).

It's not just a play on words, but it is the truth. We receive the peace of God by receiving the God of peace. This is a peace that the Qur'an and Muslims know nothing about.

PRAY FOR MUSLIMS

Jesus said, "But I say to you, Love your enemies and pray for those who persecute you" (Matthew 5:44).

Pray that millions of Muslims around the world may find the peace of Christ by turning to the true word of God. Pray that Satan would be lifted from them and their eyes would be opened to God's truth, and they would no longer be deceived by a false gospel. Pray for the protection of missionaries bringing the gospel to Muslim lands. And pray that the blood of Jesus would cut off the teaching of hatred to young Muslims.

CHRISTIANS MUST HAVE CORRECT THEOLOGY

It is important that we provide correct answers when Muslims ask questions about Christianity. One thing Muslims are told by their imams is that Christians worship three gods, while Muslims are monotheistic and worship a single god. They are referring to the Christian doctrine of the Trinity, which is mentioned by name in the Qur'an as a failing of Christianity.

The Trinity is a doctrine which has left Christian evangelists tongue-tied looking for explanations to give to unbelievers, and it has even been a stumbling block to some confessing Christians, who become confused by the many different explanations given of this doctrine. So, the next chapter will be devoted to the Trinity, and will attempt to clear the air of the unbiblical teachings which accompany this doctrine.

10
THE TRINITY DOCTRINE PRESENTS STUMBLING BLOCKS

The Trinity Defined

A common misunderstanding is that the word *Trinity* is simply a shorthand term for Father, Son, and Holy Spirit. Someone may say, "I believe in the Trinity," meaning "I believe in the Father, Son, and Holy Spirit." This is a serious misunderstanding. Trinity is a *doctrine* about who God is—an explanation of how the Father, Son, and Holy Spirit relate to one another.

An historically correct statement of the Trinity doctrine is:

> *The Trinity doctrine states that God is one God who exists simultaneously as three distinct persons: the Father, the Son, and the Holy Spirit. These three persons are coequal and coeternal.*

If the above definition confuses you, you're not alone. A Christian layman reading this may think, "Well, I guess the theologians have worked it all out, so I'll just take their word for it and go on to something more comprehensible." A non-Christian reading this may decide we Christians are a little bit off our rockers, and for good reason. The Trinity doctrine says God claims to be three different people, all at the same time. A psychologist would diagnose anyone claiming to be three persons at once as having dissociative identity disorder—in other words, as having a serious mental disease. And who wants to worship a God with a mental disease?

147

Historical Context

The doctrine of the Trinity has been around since a few hundred years after Jesus' life on earth, but it seems the internet has brought the Trinity into more prominence in recent years. Churches which once used the Apostles' Creed as their statement of faith (a creed which never mentions the Trinity), now feature websites with customized statements of belief which always seem to include the Trinity—although each church gives its own modified definition of the Trinity. The result is a confusing array of definitions of the Trinity being put forward by modern churches.

ORIGINS OF THE TRINITY DOCTRINE

The word Trinity never occurs in Scripture, and the concept is never defined in Scripture. If you were to ask any of the church's founding theologians—the Apostles Peter, John, James, and Paul—whether they believed in the Trinity, they would say, "Trinity? What is that?" And yet many churches today are telling their congregations they must believe in the Trinity to be considered Christian.

So how did the idea of the Trinity get started? It was started several generations after the time of the original Apostles, by church fathers who were searching for formulas to defend Christian orthodoxy against various heretical teachings. Their cause was a worthy cause, but the results were not always helpful to believers. These theologians were not only trained in the Bible, they were also trained in Greek philosophy. The general feeling was then (and often is today, as well) that the language of metaphysics is more rigorous and sophisticated than the language of the Bible. Therefore, biblical ideas are best defended by using the language and thinking of Greek philosophers.

The original definition of the Trinity comes from the Athanasian Creed, dated around the fourth or fifth century A.D. It is so wordy that I won't quote it here, but I have put it at the end of this chapter so you can read it if you are interested. In my researches, the best summary of what the Athanasian Creed said about the Trinity is this one, posted by James White, April 29, 1998, on the Alpha & Omega Ministries website:

> "The doctrine of the Trinity is simply that there is one eternal being of God – indivisible, infinite. This one being of God is shared by three co-equal, co-eternal persons, the Father, the Son, and the Spirit."[1]

This is short and to the point, but I can't help noting that the author then gives a lengthy explanation of the meaning. It's almost as though he is admitting to the reader, "I know this is confusing—especially that part about being indivisible and yet three different persons—so now I'll try to talk my way around it and see if I can cover up the problem with more words."

---

[1] http://www.aomin.org/aoblog/1998/04/29/a-brief-definition-of-the-trinity

Greek Thinking vs. Biblical Thinking

The idea of "three in one" is an idea from the Greek philosophers' way of thinking based on concepts derived from the material world; it is not from the biblical way based on spiritual revelation. It is a product of explaining things in terms of mathematical analogy rather than using the words of God himself. The Bible warns us that God's thinking is different from human thinking. As the Lord told Isaiah: "For my thoughts are not your thoughts, neither are your ways my ways, says the LORD. For as the heavens are higher than the earth, so are my ways higher than your ways and my thoughts than your thoughts" (Isaiah 55:8–9). We need to acknowledge the limitations of our thinking from the beginning and realize there are certain things completely hidden from our eyes unless God reveals them to us. To extend God's revelation by using the language of metaphysics will only lead to corrupted teaching and confusion.

GREEK WISDOM OPPOSED TO BIBLICAL WISDOM

Several times in the Bible, the Lord specifically identifies "Greek" thinking and "Greek" wisdom as enemies of God's divine wisdom. The apostle Paul said in his letter to the Corinthians.

> "For the word of the cross is folly to those who are perishing, but to us who are being saved it is the power of God. For it is written,

'I will destroy the wisdom of the wise, and the cleverness of the clever I will thwart.'

Where is the wise man? Where is the scribe? Where is the debater of this age? Has not God made foolish the wisdom of the world? For since, in the wisdom of God, the world did not know God through wisdom, it pleased God through the folly of what we preach to save those who believe. For Jews demand signs and Greeks seek wisdom, but we preach Christ crucified, a stumbling block to Jews and folly to Gentiles, but to those who are called, both Jews and Greeks, Christ the power of God and the wisdom of God. For the foolishness of God is wiser than men, and the weakness of God is stronger than men" (1 Corinthians 1:18–25).

He says God's wisdom appears to be foolishness in the eyes of men, because it does not conform to the Greek way of thinking. And he sets up the two kinds of wisdom—divine wisdom and Greek wisdom—as enemies of each other. This opposition becomes even clearer in the words spoken by God through Zechariah the prophet:

"I will brandish your sons, O Zion, over your sons, O Greece, and wield you like a warrior's sword" (Zechariah 9:13).

God plans to use us, his believers, to *defeat* (not *adopt*) the thinking of Greece, and to overcome it with our warrior's sword—the word of God. This is not just a statement of fact, it is a call to action. God is warning us that the thinking of the philosophers is not only different from his thinking, but is opposed to his thinking. We must choose one kind of thinking or the other. We cannot have it both ways. If we try to think of God in terms of mathematical models, we will only cause ourselves confusion and weaken our testimony to the gospel.

GOD CANNOT BE DESCRIBED BY MATHEMATICAL MODELS

The desire for a mathematical model is so strong that the Trinity is sometimes depicted by a geometric design like the one below:

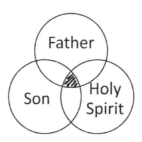

Designs like this can be seen in the stained-glass windows of some churches, and a similar design also appears on the covers of some recent editions of the New King James Bible. When you see a picture like that, you know instinctively you are dealing with false teaching. First, math—including geometry—is a tool for describing physical elements of the creation, not for describing the spiritual nature of the Creator himself. Second, what do you say about that center area of the diagram where all three lobes overlap? Is that area of overlap some super-special part of God, where God's essence is more concentrated? And does that make the outer lobes less special, containing less-concentrated doses of God? And when you pray, are you now going to think of yourself as praying to a geometric pattern? "God is spirit" (not something physical) "and those who worship him must worship in spirit and truth" (John 4:24). Attempts to picture God mathematically or geometrically betray more confusion and give an unbiblical portrayal of God.

TRINITY IMAGES VIOLATE THE SECOND COMMANDMENT

Here is another image that has been used for the Trinity:

The triangle within a circle is an ancient occult symbol. Satanists use the triangle within a circle and place an all-seeing eye at the center to represent Satan and Satan's power in the universe. Christians should be horrified at the idea of using an occult symbol to represent God, but it does not take much exploring on the internet to find it being used in Christian apologetics.

When God told us not to make any likeness or image of him (the Second Commandment, Exodus 20:4–6), he meant to include geometric shapes in that statement. We do not draw pictures of God.

The Trinity and Islam

While the word Trinity does not occur in the Bible, it *does* occur in the Qur'an (the holy book of Islam). Already in the seventh century A.D. Muhammad was citing the doctrine of the Trinity as a weakness of Christianity. He correctly sensed that if he could propose a God who was not three different persons, but just one person (that is, a God without psychological problems), his religion would have an advantage over Christianity. He could exploit the confusion Christians encountered in explaining the Trinity. Christian theologians, please note: The doctrine of the Trinity has played a role in leading millions of people away from Christianity and into slavery to a false religion.

The Trinity in Modern Statements of Belief

I mentioned that it has become common for churches to post their customized statements of belief, almost always including their own version of the doctrine of the Trinity. Let's look at three.

MODERN STATEMENTS OF BELIEF: THE UNITED METHODIST CHURCH

A new believer thinking of joining a United Methodist church might browse the United Methodist Church (UMC) website and find this statement:

> When we say the Apostles' Creed, we join
> with millions of Christians through the ages in
> an understanding of God as a Trinity—three
> persons in one: Father, Son, and Holy Spirit.
> God, who is one, is revealed in three distinct
> persons. "God in three persons, blessed Trinity"
> is one way of speaking about the several ways
> we experience God.

Did the authors of this statement bother to read the Apostles' Creed? The Apostles' Creed speaks of the Father, the Son, and the Holy Spirit, but it never mentions the three-in-one concept of the Trinity. Do the UMC authors assume simply talking about the Father, Son, and Holy Spirit is the same as postulating a doctrine of the Trinity? Apparently they are suggesting to new believers if they simply believe in the Father, Son, and Holy Spirit, then they also adhere to the doctrine of the Trinity. Theological problems are resolved simply by ignoring them.

The UMC statement says "God in three persons, blessed Trinity" is a "way of speaking" about the ways we "experience God." They are deftly and deceptively changing the Trinity from a definition of who God is, to an expression of how people experience God. But there are many ways we experience God, not just three ways. We may experience God through the beauty of a sunset, or in a newborn baby's smile, or in a helping hand from a friend, and none of these ways is considered (according to their definition) part of the Trinity. The UMC statement tricks our minds into forgetting the Trinity is a metaphysical statement of who God is.

MODERN STATEMENTS OF BELIEF: SOUTHERN BAPTIST CONVENTION

As another example, let's take a statement from the website of the Southern Baptist Convention (SBC):

> There is one and only one living and true God.
> …The eternal triune God reveals Himself to us
> as Father, Son and Holy Spirit, with distinct
> personal attributes, but without division of
> nature, essence, or being.

Does it really make any sense to speak of "one and only one" God, and then call God "triune"? In normal English, triune means having three parts, or being threefold. The SBC statement is probably an attempt to reconcile the doctrine of the Trinity with Deuteronomy 6:4, which said, "Hear, O Israel: The LORD our God is one LORD." The SBC approach is to claim he is one God, but he "reveals himself to us" in different ways. This is beginning to sound a lot like the UMC talk about "ways we experience God." Once again, it is an attempt to sidestep Trinity as a metaphysical definition of who God is, and change it into a statement that is situation-dependent—a statement meaning something like, "God speaks to us now one way, now another way."

GOD REVEALS HIMSELF IN MILLIONS OF WAYS, NOT JUST THREE

God reveals himself to us in many ways. Saying God is "triune" is not a statement about ways God reveals himself to us, it is a claim about who God is—an assertion that God's nature occurs in three parts. To say God is triune, and then say that he is "without division of nature," is incomprehensible. The SBC may try to deflect the confusion by talking about ways God reveals himself, but they are not being intellectually (or spiritually) honest.

MODERN STATEMENTS OF BELIEF: STONEBRIAR COMMUNITY CHURCH

As a third example, here is a statement from the website of Stonebriar Community Church in Frisco, Texas. This is the church of Dr. Chuck Swindoll, a well-known Christian author and radio show host. The statement reads:

We believe that the Godhead eternally exists in three persons—the Father, the Son and the Holy Spirit—and that these three are one God, having precisely the same nature, attributes, and perfections, and worthy of precisely the same homage, confidence, and obedience.

USE OF THE WORD "GODHEAD" IS A SACRILEGE

If the word Trinity is confusing, the word Godhead which is used here is downright odious. The word Godhead suggests some super-God (or especially intelligent part of God?) even more exalted than a mere God could be. Now (it seems to say) we're not just talking about God, we're talking about an even greater "Godhead." God the Father is just one of three parts of this Godhead, so the Godhead must be more important than God the Father. I ask the reader to judge: Is it blasphemy to posit a concept greater and more exalted than God the Father—a concept that reduces God the Father to a part of a greater whole? And once again there is incomprehensible talk about three separate persons who have the same "nature" and "attributes."

THE TRINITY AS SEEN BY THE FAITHFUL

What about the everyday application of these Trinitarian ideas to a Christian's faith? Does any person in the Bible, or in Stonebriar Church or any other church, *pray* to the Godhead or the Trinity? Fortunately, this seems to be rare. Jesus taught us to pray to "our Father who art in heaven"—not to a Godhead or a Trinity. There seems to be an unspoken understanding among believers that Godhead and Trinity are terms theologians like to talk about, but they have no place in our actual spiritual lives.

If a theological concept has no part in our spiritual lives, that is a sign it should be discarded.

THE WORD "COEQUAL"

The idea of complete equality among the Father, Son, and Holy Spirit has through history been a fundamental part of the doctrine of the Trinity. The Trinity doctrine—correctly stated—defines God as three *coequal* persons in one. My guess is the authors of the three church statements above may have avoided that word to forestall some uncomfortable questions. They have deliberately dumbed down their definition of the Trinity, perhaps thinking to avoid confusion, but at the cost of correctness.

Coequality is an essential part of the Trinity doctrine. We will see a little further on, however, how Scripture refutes the idea of coequality.

The Holy Spirit is Not a Person

The Trinity doctrine asserts that the Holy Spirit is the "third person" of the Trinity. But as we study scripture, we find the Holy Spirit is not a person at all, but is better defined as the breath of God—the breath of God coming forth from God's mouth with power to perform his will. Obviously, if the Holy Spirit is not a person, the Holy Spirit cannot be the third person of the Trinity.

In the Old Testament, the Hebrew word "ruah" is used for Spirit, and ruah—the very same word—also means breath or wind. In the New Testament, the Greek word "pneuma" is used for Spirit, and it too has the alternate meanings of breath or wind. These definitions are significant, because people reading Scripture in the original languages would always, in all contexts, be aware of the association of spirit with breath—an association lost in English translations.

OLD TESTAMENT EXAMPLE: GOD BREATHES HIS SPIRIT INTO THE DRY BONES

A famous example that illustrates the multiple meanings of the word ruah occurs in Ezekiel chapter 37—the vision of the dry bones. At one point Ezekiel sees a vision of a valley filled with lifeless bodies lying on the valley floor. Then God says to Ezekiel:

>"'Prophesy to the breath, prophesy, son of man, and say to the breath, Thus says the Lord GOD: Come from the four winds, O breath, and breathe upon these slain, that they may live.' So I prophesied as he commanded me, and the breath came into them, and they lived, and stood upon their feet, an exceedingly great host" (Ezekiel 37:9–10).

The word translated as "breath" is ruah. Here you can see ruah is associated with wind (the same word ruah is used), and it is associated with God's life-giving Spirit, since it gives life to the dead bodies. A few verses later, the Lord explains the meaning of the vision to Ezekiel. It is a message to the people of Israel who have given up hope. God addresses the people, and says to them, "And I will put my Spirit within you, and you shall live, and I will place you in your own land; then you shall know that I, the LORD, have spoken, and I have done it, says the LORD" (Ezekiel 37:14). Here the word for Spirit is again ruah—the breath of God.

NEW TESTAMENT EXAMPLE: THE HOLY SPIRIT COMES AS A WIND AND TONGUES OF FLAME

A famous passage in the New Testament brings out the triple meaning of the word "pneuma." It occurs in Acts chapter 2, the story of the Holy Spirit coming upon the disciples on the Day of Pentecost.

>"When the day of Pentecost had come, they were all together in one place. And suddenly a sound came from heaven like the rush of a

mighty wind, and it filled all the house where they were sitting. And there appeared to them tongues as of fire, distributed and resting on each one of them. And they were all filled with the Holy Spirit and began to speak in other tongues, as the Spirit gave them utterance" (Acts 2:1–4).

Here the Holy Spirit (pneuma) is heard arriving like the rush of a mighty wind (pneuma)—it's the same word. And then the Spirit is associated with breath and speech in the disciples themselves, as it inspires the disciples to speak God's praises in new languages.

THE HOLY SPIRIT AS COUNSELOR

There are some Bible passages, however, where the Holy Spirit appears in other forms, and a few of these passages from the gospel of John are often invoked as proof that the Holy Spirit is a person (the third person of the Trinity). In one of these passages (John 14:26) Jesus says to his disciples: "But the Counselor, the Holy Spirit, whom the Father will send in my name, he will teach you all things, and bring to your remembrance all that I have said to you." Some theologians conclude that since the Holy Spirit in this passage is a *he*, the Holy Spirit must be a person, and since the Holy Spirit is a person, the Holy Spirit must be the third person of the Trinity. This involves the assumption, however, that where there is a voice there must be a body, since a person has to have a body. But the Counselor sent by Jesus never manifests itself in bodily form.

THE HOLY SPIRIT IN OTHER FORMS

There are Bible passages where the Holy Spirit takes yet other, non-person forms. When Jesus was baptized by John the Baptist, "the Holy Spirit descended upon him [Jesus] in bodily form, as a dove" (Luke 3:22). Since the Holy Spirit descended as a dove, should we conclude the Holy Spirit is a dove, and the Trinity consists of two persons plus a dove? That would be a ridiculous conclusion no one is likely to draw. And recall the passage about Pentecost, where the Holy Spirit appeared in tongues of flame. Does that mean the Trinity must be two persons plus a tongue of flame? No one is likely to draw that conclusion. What we see overall in Scripture is the Holy Spirit is normally associated with *breath* or *wind* from God (the word is the same for all three), but sometimes takes other forms as God directs. One of those other forms then is the Counselor (also translated as Advisor or Helper) in the passage from John 14. The Holy Spirit takes that form because it is so directed by God the Father in particular circumstances, not because it is a third person of the Trinity.

NO SEAT IN HEAVEN FOR THE HOLY SPIRIT

We know when Jesus was resurrected he was given a seat at the right hand of the throne of God (Hebrews 8:1). But nowhere is it said there is a seat in heaven for the Holy Spirit. There never has been, and never will be, a seat for the Holy Spirit, because the Holy Spirit is not a person to take a seat. And if the Holy Spirit is not a person, then it cannot be the third person of the Trinity.

The Father and Son are Not Coequal

So instead of a Trinity, are we now left with a Duality? Are we left with a God who consists of two parts—a Son and a Father? Two parts may be more reasonable than three parts, but talking about a God who is both his own son and his own father still sounds like a psychological disorder. And it still comes up against the statement in Deuteronomy 6:4 where Moses proclaims, "Hear, O Israel: The LORD our God is one LORD."

PAUL NEVER SAID "COEQUAL"

The doctrine of the Trinity claims that the three persons of the Trinity are coequal. There is a passage from Paul's letter to the Colossians which might seem to buttress arguments for Jesus and the Father being coequal. It reads:

> "He [Jesus] is the image of the invisible God, the first-born of all creation; for in him all things were created, in heaven and on earth, visible and invisible, whether thrones or dominions or principalities or authorities—all things were created through him and for him. He is before all things, and in him all things hold together. He is the head of the body, the church; he is the beginning, the first-born from the dead, that in everything he might be pre-

eminent. For in him all the fulness of God was pleased to dwell, and through him to reconcile to himself all things, whether on earth or in heaven, making peace by the blood of his cross" (Colossians 1:15–20).

Paul was searching for all the right words to describe the relationship between Jesus and the Father, and while he was familiar with Greek thinking, he never used the word *coequal*—not here, and not in any other place in Scripture.

JESUS BORE THE IMAGE OF GOD

In the passage, Paul first uses the word *image*, saying Jesus is "the image of the invisible God." This is a reminder of a conversation between Jesus and his disciple Philip, in which Philip asked Jesus to show them the Father. Jesus answered him, "Have I been with you so long, and yet you do not know me, Philip? He who has seen me has seen the Father; how can you say, 'Show us the Father'?" (John 14:9). Here Jesus obviously did not mean seeing him was the same as ascending into heaven and seeing God sitting in glory on his throne. What Jesus meant (to paraphrase) was: "All you need to know about God is visible to you in my every word and every action, because everything I do and say is in direct obedience to God." Everything Jesus said and did bore God's likeness.

ALL THE FULLNESS OF GOD

Then Paul states "all the fullness of God" came to dwell within Jesus. This carries forward the idea of Jesus doing everything in exact obedience to God, but adds to it the understanding Jesus did not perform God's will like a mechanical robot, but acted

165

because his every wish and heart's desire was the same as the Father's.

JESUS SUBORDINATE TO GOD

Paul says "all things were created *through* him [Jesus] and *for* him"—but not *by* him. There is here still an implicit subordination of Jesus to the Father: All things were created *by* the Father, through the Son. If we examine other passages, we find a similar subordination appearing. For example, Hebrews 8:6 speaks of Jesus as having a *ministry*: "But as it is, Christ has obtained a ministry which is as much more excellent than the old as the covenant he mediates is better, since it is enacted on better promises." A minister is an agent of someone else. Jesus is acting as an agent of the Father. An agent is understood to be subordinate to the one he represents.

Several Bible verses refer to Jesus as a *mediator*. Hebrews 9:15 calls Jesus "the mediator of a new covenant," and 1 Timothy 2:5 says, "For there is one God, and there is one mediator between God and men, the man Christ Jesus." This latter statement puts God and Jesus at different levels. The picture suggested is of God seated on his throne as judge, with Jesus as the lawyer mediating between his client (us) and the judge (God). Lawyer and judge are both way above us, but they are not coequal with each other.

MAKES NO SENSE TO SAY JESUS PRAYED TO HIMSELF

The Bible tells us Jesus would go out to a desert place and spend long hours praying to God. If Jesus and the Father are both, well, God, then what sense does it make for Jesus to spend long hours praying to God? Wouldn't it be very odd for him to be praying to himself—praying not just in a symbolic way, but in such earnest petition that at one point he was sweating drops of blood? Jesus most definitely was not praying to another form of himself, and when Scripture says he was obedient to the Father, it doesn't mean he was simply being obedient to another form of himself. In that case, his obedience wouldn't mean much.

The book of Hebrews tells us:

> "In the days of his flesh, Jesus offered up prayers and supplications, with loud cries and tears, to him who was able to save him from death, and he was heard for his godly fear. Although he was a Son, he learned obedience through what he suffered; and being made perfect he became the source of eternal salvation to all who obey him, being designated by God a high priest after the order of Melchiz'edek" (Hebrews 5:7–10).

OBEDIENCE TO SOMEONE IMPLIES SUBORDINATION

The distress Jesus endured was not in obedience to himself, or some form of himself; it was in obedience to his Father in heaven. How could he be obedient to God without being subordinate to him? And according to this passage, Jesus "learned obedience." Wouldn't it be odd to say God "learned" anything, since God knows all things? And this passage says Jesus was "made perfect." It would be blasphemy to say God had to be made perfect, since God himself is the definition of perfection.

THE "SON HIMSELF WILL ALSO BE SUBJECTED TO" THE FATHER

A passage in 1 Corinthians even more forcefully contradicts the idea of the first two persons of the Trinity being "coequal." In this passage, Paul is speaking of the resurrected Jesus.

> "'For God has put all things in subjection under his [Jesus'] feet.' But when it says, 'All things are put in subjection under him,' it is plain that he is excepted who put all things under him. When all things are subjected to him, then the Son himself will also be subjected to him who put all things under him, that God may be everything to every one" (1 Corinthians 15:27–28).

Paul here makes it clear the Son will "be subjected" to God the Father. In fact, *everything* will be subjected to God the Father. *There is no such thing as coequality with God.*

What About John 1:1?

John 1:1 is sometimes used as a proof text for the Trinity Doctrine. The verse is first quoted: "In the beginning was the Word, and the Word was with God, and the Word was God"—then is followed by the observation that since the Word refers to Jesus, this means Jesus is God. "The Word was God" becomes "the Word is God." Past tense becomes present tense, and the transition from past to present is not noticed or explained.

But the distinction between past and present is important here. Just as you might say you "were" your father at a time before you were conceived (when you were still "in the loins" of your father, to use the biblical expression), so John could say that Jesus (the Word) "was God" in a time way back at the beginning, before Jesus became the Son. God intends for us not to speculate about the process by which Jesus became the Son. All we know for sure is that a father precedes the son, and the son proceeds from the father. (Compare John 8:42, where Jesus said "I proceeded and came forth from God.") So Jesus "was God" at that primordial time "in the beginning," in a sense similar to that in which human sons at some original point "are" their father. But that does not mean we should say today "Jesus is God," any more than you or I would say today "I am my father."

John is making the important distinction between being a Son and being some creature of God's creation. When John says "the Word was God," he does it to emphasize that God **really is related to Jesus as** *Father*—**God is not simply Jesus'** *creator*.

And Jesus really is related to God as the Son—he proceeded from his Father. He is not one of God's created beings, like all the other denizens of heaven and earth.

A Correct Understanding

The Trinity and the Godhead are concepts arising out of metaphysical ways of thinking. But God has warned us we can't use metaphysics (Greek philosophical thinking) to understand heavenly things. Confused Christians, take heart. If you can't quite wrap your mind around the concepts of the Trinity and the Godhead, that is a good sign. It means your brain is rebelling against a teaching that is false. It means when you read the commandment to "love the Lord your God with all your heart, and with all your soul, and with all your mind" (Matthew 22:37), you instinctively rebel against the idea of loving some three-part, metaphysical construct not mentioned in your Bible.

WHAT THEN IS A CORRECT UNDERSTANDING OF FATHER, SON, AND HOLY SPIRIT?

So what is the proper response when we are asked if we believe in the Trinity? We may say simply, *"I believe that God is the Father, Jesus is the Son, and the Holy Spirit is the very breath of God."* And by saying that, we avoid long-winded philosophical discussions about a non-biblical concept that can only create confusion. Much better to refrain from using the word Trinity altogether.

PLEASE DO NOT SAY "GOD THE FATHER, GOD THE SON, AND GOD THE HOLY SPIRIT"

What if you're a member of the clergy, preparing a statement of faith? There's no harm in falling back on the Apostles' Creed, which is short, to the point, and says nothing about the Trinity. But if you must compose something unique, please do not do like the Southern Baptist Convention and title three sections of your statement "God the Father," "God the Son," and "God the Holy Spirit." To those of us not mesmerized by theological jargon, that seems to be naming three separate gods. It seems to be naming three gods because that is exactly what it does: It lists three gods, one after the other. To curious Muslims who might be investigating Christianity, the warnings of their teachers will be confirmed. Correct statements would be:

God is the Father,

Jesus is the Son of God, and

The Holy Spirit is the very breath of God.

All we need to know is contained in those statements.

Addendum: Athanasian Creed
(Fourth or Fifth Century A.D.)

Here is the part of the Athanasian Creed dealing with the Trinity. Note that the word "catholic" does not refer to the Roman Catholic Church, but means the universal church of all Christians.

We worship one God in trinity and the Trinity in unity, neither confusing the persons nor dividing the divine being. For the Father is one person, the Son is another, and the Spirit is still another. But the deity of the Father, Son, and Holy Spirit is one, equal in glory, coeternal in majesty. What the Father is, the Son is, and so is the Holy Spirit. Uncreated is the Father; uncreated is the Son; uncreated is the Spirit. The Father is infinite; the Son is infinite; the Holy Spirit is infinite. Eternal is the Father; eternal is the Son; eternal is the Spirit: And yet there are not three eternal beings, but one who is eternal; as there are not three uncreated and unlimited beings, but one who is uncreated and unlimited. Almighty is the Father; almighty is the Son; almighty is the Spirit: And yet there are not three almighty beings, but one who is almighty. Thus the Father is God; the Son is God; the Holy Spirit is God: And yet there are not three gods, but one God. Thus the Father is Lord; the Son is Lord; the Holy Spirit is Lord: And yet there are not three lords, but one Lord. As Christian truth compels us to acknowledge each distinct person as God and Lord, so catholic religion forbids us to say that there are three gods or lords. The Father was neither made nor created nor begotten; the Son was neither made nor created, but was alone begotten of the Father; the Spirit was neither made nor created, but is proceeding from the Father and the Son. Thus there is one Father, not three fathers; one Son, not three sons; one Holy Spirit, not three spirits. And in this Trinity, no one is before or after, greater or less than the other; but all three persons are in themselves, coeternal and coequal; and so we must worship the Trinity in unity and the one God in three persons. Whoever wants to be saved should think thus about the Trinity. It is necessary for eternal salvation that one also faithfully believe that our Lord Jesus Christ became flesh.[2]

---

2   https://www.gotquestions.org/Athanasian-creed.html, used by permission

PART TWO

UNDERSTANDING THE WORDS

Revelation chapter 12 records a vision in which Satan appears as a serpent-dragon, and God's church is portrayed as a woman being pursued by the dragon. Part of the vision reads like this:

> "The serpent poured water like a river out of his mouth after the woman, to sweep her away with the flood. But the earth came to the help of the woman, and the earth opened its mouth and swallowed the river which the dragon had poured from his mouth. Then the dragon was angry with the woman, and went off to make war on the rest of her offspring, on those who keep the commandments of God and bear testimony to Jesus. And he stood on the sand of the sea" (Revelation 12:15–17).

The flood from the dragon's mouth is the flood of lies and deceptions we are experiencing now in America. It's a flood of words. Satan wants to sweep us away with false teaching.

The vision says the earth helped the woman by swallowing the river of deceptions. We see all around us people who are intelligent and well-meaning swallowing the deceptions of Satan. We wonder sometimes how they can be so deceived, but we know the answer. The answer is, the Spirit of Jesus and the word of God are absent from their lives. They are spiritually blinded by Satan.

The vision next states, "the dragon was angry with the woman [God's believers], and went off to make war on the rest of her offspring, on those who keep the commandments of God and bear testimony to Jesus." We are being tested to see if we will fall for the deceptions, or if we will remain true to the word of God. Every lie we accept becomes a wedge to separate us from God.

The coming chapters tell a story of the words—not the events—which define modern American culture. There is here no retelling of civil rights demonstrations or of legislative battles, but a history of some keywords that determine the way Americans think about themselves and about their country.

We will show how Satan takes familiar words and twists them to deceive us, and how at the same time God's word undercuts Satan's lies. For believers, God's word becomes a dam against the flood. The apostle James reminds us it is not easy, but the prize is of infinite worth: "Blessed is the man who endures trial, for when he has stood the test he will receive the crown of life which God has promised to those who love him" (James 1:12). Trials do not only come in the form of physical persecution, but in the form of false teaching—in the form of words.

11
THOMAS JEFFERSON AND THE
AMERICAN MYTH OF EQUALITY

The Bible Contradicts
Thomas Jefferson

Americans are taught from an early age to regard Thomas Jefferson's words in the Declaration of Independence as sacrosanct: "We hold these truths to be self-evident, that all men are created equal." I've never heard a minister question those words, and yet the Bible directly contradicts them. For example, when Isaac's wife Rebekah was pregnant with twins Jacob and Esau, the Lord told her: "Two nations are in your womb, and two peoples, born of you, shall be divided; the one shall be stronger than the other, the elder shall serve the younger" (Genesis 25:23). Jacob and Esau were created unequal, and their inequality was foreordained by God. And notice that this inequality is not a simple inequality of abilities, as if one were destined to be a gifted musician and the other a carpenter. It is a *social* inequality—"the elder shall serve the younger"—which is part of God's plan.

As another example, in both the Old and New Testament, the father is designated as head of the family, and is charged with teaching God's laws to the family. Children are to honor and obey their parents. Equality between sexes (again, referring to *social* equality), and equality between generations, are both out of the question, because God has ordained a structure to the family.

INEQUALITY IS PART OF GOD'S PLAN

Does God have a reason for inequality? In the New Testament, Paul likened the Christian church to a human body with many unequal parts, in which all parts must perform their respective, God-given functions in order for the body as a whole to function. Paul said:

> "But as it is, God arranged the organs in the body, each one of them, as he chose. If all were a single organ, where would the body be? As it is, there are many parts, yet one body. The eye cannot say to the hand, 'I have no need of you,' nor again the head to the feet, 'I have no need of you.' ... But God has so composed the body, giving the greater honor to the inferior part, that there may be no discord in the body, but that the members may have the same care for one another. If one member suffers, all suffer together; if one member is honored, all rejoice together" (1 Corinthians 12:18–21, 24–26).

No two people, not even identical twins, have ever been created equal. Inequality is part of God's plan, so that many different parts—not just in the church, but in society—contribute their essential functions to the entire body.

A MYSTERIOUS PART OF GOD'S PLAN

In Acts 17, Paul is trying to explain to the Greeks how they are included in God's plan, even though they have not been given God's Scripture like the Jews. Paul tells them God "made from one every nation of men to live on all the face of the earth, having determined allotted periods and the boundaries of their habitation, that they should seek God, in the hope that they might feel after him and find him" (Acts 17:26–27).

God's purpose in making different nations, in different times and different places, is that they should *seek* him and *feel after* him and *find* him. It is no coincidence that at the same time our society is trying to erase differences among people and say that all people are equal, we are also trying to erase all memory of God.

I am calling this part of God's plan a mystery because it is not obvious why differences among people should cause them to call on God. We may think if we were in God's place we would not do it that way. The best clue to solving the mystery is probably in the story of the city of Babel in Genesis. The people proposed to build "a city, and a tower with its top in the heavens" in order to "make a name for" themselves (Genesis 11:4).

> "And the LORD said, 'Behold, they are one people, and they have all one language; and this is only the beginning of what they will do; and nothing that they propose to do will now be impossible for them. Come, let us go down, and there confuse their language, that they may not understand one another's speech.' So the LORD scattered them abroad from there over the face of all the earth, and they left off building the city" (Genesis 11:6–8).

Before God scattered the people, they threatened to vaunt themselves against God. Their power and self-importance were becoming so great that they would become gods in their own minds and in their control over earth. They would worship themselves, not God. It is worth remembering that it was their technology—their ability with bricks and mortar—that led them to challenge God's authority by building their tall tower. Could there be a parallel with our modern technology? our ability to build tall towers? our plans to become a multi-planet species?

EQUAL JUSTICE

It is important for us to uphold the principle that all men—rich or poor, black or white—are entitled to equal justice before the law. "You shall not have in your house two kinds of measures, a large and a small" (Deuteronomy 25:14). God's law says equal justice is to apply across the board to all, whether rich or poor: "You shall not be partial to the poor or defer to the great, but in righteousness shall you judge your neighbor" (Leviticus 19:15). This kind of equality is firmly established in God's word.

But equal justice does not mean all men are created equal. Jefferson said his ideas about equality were "self-evident," meaning his ideas were not based on the Bible, and not on any outside authority, but on his own thinking. It is also telling that Jefferson's Bible (now carefully preserved at the Smithsonian Institution as a kind of national treasure) reveals major sections carved out by Jefferson's penknife and discarded. In other words, Jefferson placed himself in a position of authority over the word of God. He placed his own word ahead of the word of God.

But we know the real authority for how men are created lies with the Creator himself. It is up to God, the Creator, to decide whether men are created equal. It is not up to Thomas Jefferson, or you, or me, or anyone else.

In Reality, the American Way Opposes Equality

While we Americans bandy the word equality about, the thing we've been most proud of (until now) is our individual *inequality*. I'm talking about the American ideals of individual achievement, do your own thing, be all that you can be, pull yourself up by your bootstraps, etc.—ideals which make us a land of opportunity, *a land for individuals to rise and show how unequal they are*. In the popular mythology, this means placing a high value on self-realization: I become the self-made man or woman of my dreams, and I do so by proudly setting my own rules. "I did it my way," the famous American song proclaims.

Think about this: Does anybody in America, male or female, black or white, want to be equal to somebody else? No, we want to show our uniqueness. And even if we wanted to be equal, would equality be possible? No, because no two people are created equal. That's the way God made us, like it or not. America prospers more than any other country in the world because it encourages everyone to take their unique *inequalities* and make them shine.

How do Christians fit into this American scenario of individual achievement and self-realization? The popular version of self-realization is intended to focus on self—to turn hearts away from God. The American myth tells us we can do it all on our own power and we don't need God. But for Christians, it is different. For Christians, America does not represent an opportunity for self-realization, but for realization of our place in God's plan. In America, we have an opportunity to be "the best we can be"—not by proudly creating our own rules, but by showing our complete obedience to God's rules. We trust by so doing, we will each take our unique, individual place within God's plan, and so bring glory to his name.

12
MARTIN LUTHER KING, JR., AND EQUALITY

The "I Have a Dream" Speech

In American schools today, the Rev. Dr. Martin Luther King, Jr. is probably held in even higher esteem than Thomas Jefferson. King's rhetoric, however, is based on the words of Thomas Jefferson. In King's famous "I Have a Dream" speech, King quotes Jefferson, saying it is his dream all Americans will learn to live out the American creed which proclaims, "all men are created equal." So King attaches his dream firmly to the Jeffersonian myth of equality.

King also quotes the Bible in his speech, suggesting to the listener that his dream has the authority of divine truth. However, just as Jefferson's statement "all men are created equal" was from Jefferson's mind, so King's dream was from King's mind, not from God. We know King was not a true representative of the Lord because of things he said which contradict the gospel, and because of the ungodly lifestyle which he led. In King's other speeches he denied the virgin birth and he claimed the physical resurrection of Jesus was not an important belief. So we know King doubted some of the most fundamental tenets of Christianity. And King's lifestyle was not the lifestyle of a God-fearing man. He had multiple extra-marital affairs and mistresses, attended orgiastic parties, and committed extensive plagiarism in his doctoral dissertation at Boston University. These are not the actions of someone trying to honor God.

There is also clear evidence from within the "I Have a Dream" speech itself that King's words are not from God. An example would be in his rousing finale, where King looks to "that day when all of God's children, black men and white men, Jews and Gentiles, Protestants and Catholics, will be able to join hands and sing in the words of the old Negro spiritual, 'Free at last! Free at last! Thank God Almighty, we are free at last!'" A true Christian minister would proclaim real freedom comes only by surrendering one's life to Jesus Christ, not through (as King puts it) "faith [in a] beautiful symphony of brotherhood." And a true Christian minister would know that according to the Bible God does *not* consider all men to be his true children, but only those who call in faith upon God's Son, Jesus Christ.

In the Bible, many men had dreams, but only some dreams were from God. The Lord once told the prophet Jeremiah what he thought of prophets who told dreams from their own mind:

> "I have heard what the prophets have said
> who prophesy lies in my name, saying, 'I have
> dreamed, I have dreamed!' How long shall
> there be lies in the heart of the prophets who
> prophesy lies, and who prophesy the deceit of
> their own heart, who think to make my people
> forget my name by their dreams which they
> tell one another, even as their fathers forgot
> my name for Ba'al? Let the prophet who has
> a dream tell the dream, but let him who has
> my word speak my word faithfully. What has
> straw in common with wheat? says the LORD.
> Is not my word like fire, says the LORD, and
> like a hammer which breaks the rock in pieces?
> Therefore, behold, I am against the prophets,
> says the LORD, who steal my words from one
> another" (Jeremiah 23:25–30).

King has joined the ranks of those false prophets who say, "I have dreamed. I have dreamed." But their dream is made of lies from their own heart. As the Lord told Jeremiah, they "think to make my people forget my name by their dreams which they tell one another." King has made himself the heir of the false prophets of Jeremiah's time. Think about this: Whose name is remembered in our schools today—the name of God or the name of Martin Luther King, Jr.? God's name has been completely erased from our schools, while King's name is everywhere.

SOCIAL JUSTICE

One may argue we should not criticize King's speech since it served the good end of bringing attention to social injustices. King's call for for equality, however, leads to invidious comparisons between people who are unequal (who were *created* unequal, like it or not) which leads to jealousy and resentment, which sow the seeds of hatred. By veering from solid scriptural teaching, King was inadvertently giving fuel to the hatred he claimed to oppose.

If there are injustices in society, then the perpetrators of the crimes should be brought to justice. *But inequality is not equivalent to injustice.* One is not likely to achieve justice by starting with an incorrect definition of the word. God gave Moses a prescient warning against modern "woke" justice when he said, "Nor shall you be partial to a poor man in his lawsuit" (Exodus 23:3).

If kindness, gentleness, and mutual respect are missing in society, then the gospel message needs to be presented to change people's hearts. But again, King's speech did not present the gospel of Jesus Christ. In its place, he preached a gospel of the universal brotherhood of all mankind—a gospel which says men *do not* need repentance and the saving blood of Jesus. All they need is a warm-hearted consciousness of their fellow man.

The requirement for equality only leads to envy and finger pointing, which generate hatred. So grievances fester until the top blows off. And this, unfortunately, is the result some people want to achieve (see, for example, the chapter on Black Lives Matter).

13
EQUALITY TEACHING SOWS
RACIAL HATRED

Media Deliberately
Incite Hatred

The words "racism" and "racist"—as used in American media today—are impostors. Those words pretend to point out instances of hatred, while their real purpose is to *create* hatred. Their purpose is to use the deceptive claims of equality to allow people to point the finger at others and denounce them.

About two and a half years into the Trump administration, a secret recording was made of a meeting of the *New York Times* editorial staff. At this meeting, the editor-in-chief congratulated the staff on having concentrated their efforts over the past two and a half years on the subject of Russian collusion by President Trump. Now, the editor said, it was time to change gears and focus on a new subject—racism. In other words, the *Times* was not reporting the news; the *Times* was creating the news. It turned out the *Times* was creating more than news—it was creating a social movement.

News organizations across the country picked up the theme immediately, and racism became the central subject of the day. Soon we began hearing scholarly-sounding terms like critical race theory and intersectionality and the 1619 Project. The 1619 Project is a K-12 educational curriculum based on the idea that racism has always been the defining characteristic of America. 1619 was the year slaves were first brought to America, and so they say that year was more important than 1776. It did not take long for the 1619 Project curriculum to be adopted by thousands of schools across the U.S.

Our children are being taught to hate America and to hate themselves for being born in America. Racism teaching is combined with teaching about oppression of other so-called minorities and leads students to think if America were destroyed it would be a good thing. Students are not allowed to ask, "Where would I be without America?"

In addition to lies about history, there are psychological lie and theological lies embedded in racism teaching. The psychological lie is that there is some group consciousness that we participate in by being born into a certain group. The theological lie is that there is a group guilt (in this instance, the guilt of white racism) which we inherit as part of our group consciousness. The Bible strongly contradicts these ideas. In both the Old Testament and the New Testament, prophets tell us that on the Day of the Lord each individual will appear before the throne of God to be judged according to what he or she has done in this life, and judgment will be according to God's standards—not according to human standards. There is no group consciousness, there is no group guilt, and there is no judgment based on group or race.

Whether the 1619 Project provides students with accurate history is not important—from the point of view of its authors, that is. Good history was never the main purpose of the 1619 Project, any more than good journalism was the main purpose of the news outlets that began to emphasize racism. The real purpose of the racism theme began to appear when some black ministers withdrew from the Southern Baptist Conference because some white ministers had rejected critical race theory. Bingo. Bitter divisions were occurring as different groups pointed the finger at one another. Division, accusations, and hatred: That was—and remains—the real goal of those who beat the drums of racism.

Races are Different

Anyone who watches sports can see there are many blacks with athletic abilities which no whites have (think 100-meter dash at the Olympics), and there are many whites with athletic abilities which no blacks have (think Tour de France bike race). No sports commentator will ever mention these obvious facts, for fear of being called racist. The shibboleth of equality has put shackles on our minds.

"Racial stereotyping" has come to be the equivalent (in the public forum) of racism. But just as Paul described various members of the Christian community as having different roles which functioned together like the organs of a body, so some racial "stereotypes" have worked to benefit our society. For example, many generations of Irishmen of New York City have served as policemen and firemen to keep New York residents safe. Many Chinese have fed and clothed Americans with their restaurants and laundries. White women schoolteachers and librarians have trained our kids. Black musicians brought us jazz music. Instead of calling these accomplishment racial stereotypes, perhaps we should call them racial gifts to all of society.

It will never help us deal with reality if we insist on pretending there are no differences between races. It will never help us deal with reality—a reality created by God, not by our wishful thinking—if we insist on pretending all people and all races are created equal.

Is God Racist?

Why does God make us this way? Does this mean God *favors* one race over another? Is God racist?

The Jews of Jesus' time considered their race to be the race favored by God. They were the people chosen by God to receive God's holy Scripture and to preserve right worship traditions. They considered all non-Jews as unclean. Jesus, however, gave them this warning:

> "But in truth, I tell you, there were many widows in Israel in the days of Elijah, when the heaven was shut up three years and six months, when there came a great famine over all the land; and Elijah was sent to none of them but only to Zarephath, in the land of Sidon, to a woman who was a widow. And there were many lepers in Israel in the time of the prophet Elisha; and none of them was cleansed, but only Na'aman the Syrian." (Luke 4:25–27)

In other words, Jesus gave them examples from Scripture of God favoring a Gentile over Jews. This idea made the Jews listening to Jesus so angry, they tried to stone Jesus. They formed a first century lynch mob. But Jesus evaded them and went on to die on the cross for the salvation of all men, of all races—

equally. That's how much God loves people of all races—he sent his beloved Son to die in their place. Jesus testifies there is no greater love than this, that a man lay down his life for his friends (John 15:13). And God's provision for the salvation of people from all races is not an afterthought, but was part of God's plan from the beginning. God prophesied of his Son through Isaiah hundreds of years before Jesus' ministry: "It is too light a thing that you should be my servant to raise up the tribes of Jacob and to restore the preserved of Israel; I will give you as a light to the nations, that my salvation may reach to the end of the earth" (Isaiah 49:6). There is no nation—no race—that Jesus' salvation does not reach.

14
RACISM, EQUITY, AND WOKENESS

"Equality" Gives Place
to "Equity"

In the 2020's it became fashionable among left-leaning speakers to use the word equity in place of equality. At the same time they gave equity a new definition. They replaced the dictionary definition of equity—freedom from bias or favoritism—with a definition meaning something like "exercise whatever bias may be necessary to satisfy the claims of a minority group."

Those who were more right-leaning had long argued that equality meant equal opportunity for all—standards were to be applied in a colorblind fashion. In other words, go by the historical definition of equity. The problem was (from the point of view of the left-leaning group) colorblind standards were not producing the desired result. Colorblind standards were not resulting in black people and other minorities being put in positions of power and influence in sufficient numbers. The argument was that prestigious positions in government, education and commerce should be filled by representatives of the various minority groups in proportion to their numbers in the overall population. White males were overrepresented in such positions. This constituted oppression by white males and created resentment among minorities.

In the black community, the words *woke* and *wokeness* arose to describe a sense that there was a plot on the part of white males to dominate and take advantage of black people, and black people had better wake up to their situation and do something about it. Soon wokeness expanded in meaning and began to be applied to other minority groups, indicating their new awareness of being oppressed by white males. Wokeness became a partner with equity. If you were woke, you were aware of the need for equity in society; you were aware of the need for minorities to replace white males in leadership positions, with credentials and abilities being of secondary consideration.

EXAMPLE: UNITED AIRLINES

On April 7, 2021, United Airlines released this statement:

> "Our flight deck should reflect the diverse group of people onboard our planes every day. That's why we plan for 50% of the 5,000 pilots we train in the next decade to be women or people of color."

This is equity in action. It is tortured logic. Why should the people flying a plane be the same as the people riding in the plane? The same logic would mean that people building bridges should be the same as people crossing the bridge, people cooking spaghetti should be the same as people eating the spaghetti, and so forth. How can a society function on such a principle? We all have different abilities which God has given us—abilities which should be for the benefit of all.

Equity is Equality Through Subtraction

There are a couple of ways you can make a group of three tennis balls equal to a group of two tennis balls: either you can add one tennis ball to the group of two, or you can subtract one ball from the group of three. Equity chooses to subtract one from the group of three. Equity is equality through subtraction.

Here's a human example. Players in the NBA are about 80% black and 20% other. Suppose it were mandated that at least 50% of players had to be white for the sake of equity. The quality of play would go down and ticket sales would decrease. Furthermore, talented black players who were excluded on the basis of racial quotas would become resentful. This would cause controversy and bad publicity for the NBA. The NBA would have achieved equality by subtraction. Equity would have reduced the value of their end product.

United Airlines should think about this example. What will happen to their pilot standards? And what will it cost them to train laymen as opposed to men who have experience flying in the military? Will they have to raise ticket prices? Society also should think about this example. What will happen to families if mothers are busy flying planes? Problems with child discipline are often related to a fatherless home—what will be the result when homes are also motherless? Equality by subtraction weakens everyone.

Critical Race Theory to
the Rescue

Critical race theory (CRT) says race is not biological but is a concept created by white people to oppress people of color. And yes, proponents of CRT use the terms "white" and "people of color" while they are denying that race is real. It is hard to know how to reply to such mind-bending logic, other than to say it defies common sense.

CRT says racism is an everyday experience for people of color, racism is embedded in our social system, and the system does not change because it benefits white people who conspire to keep the system the way it is. The implied solution is for white people to un-invent the concept of race which they previously invented. People would apparently no longer be allowed to look in a mirror and see what color their skin is, nor would they be allowed to see the color of other people's skin.

Oh, but wait a minute—CRT also says this (colorblindness) can't happen either, because then people would be judged only on the merits of what they do and say, and we would have a meritocracy. And we can't have a meritocracy because equity requires us to tip the scales in favor of blacks to compensate for past harm done by whites. Therefore we need to be able to identify races in order to adjust the scales, and ... around it goes, in circular logic.

But the true picture is simpler. There is such a thing as race, because race is a biological fact, and race is a part of every person's identity.

Aspects of Personal Identity

GROUP IDENTITY

One way we realize our identity is from associating ourselves with the achievements of other people in our "group." When a small South American country wins soccer's World Cup, everyone in the country experiences a boost in pride. Everyone in the country gets a morale boost because they can identify with their country's team and feel like they have a more important place in the world.

Racial identity is a kind of group identity. Black people don't want to see more black people as airline pilots—or CEOs or sports stars or movie stars or other positions of high visibility—because they think blacks would necessarily do a better job in those positions. They want more blacks as airline pilots (for example) because it would help them identify with the airline, with the airport, and with their country if they could see more people like themselves in positions of authority. They would have a feeling of belonging. Their identity would be more connected with everything around them. They would have black pride.

PERSONAL ACHIEVEMENTS

We also build identity through our personal achievements, by finding out what we are good at. If blacks are going to achieve equity by addition rather than subtraction, they are going to have to be good at things. Many blacks realize this, and they complain that there is systemic racism (standards tilted toward whites built into the system) which prevents them from reaching their goals.

Education is the key here. Important jobs require education. That requirement is not a sinister plot by white people. It is simply a fact that engineers have to do complex calculations, accountants have to deal accurately with lots of numbers, journalists have to master grammar and spelling, and airline pilots have to understand the complex workings of an airplane. Even blue collar workers have to keep records of expenses and income and be able to deal with taxes. These are facts of life regardless of race.

Blacks face a stark reality. According to Heather MacDonald (*The Diversity Dilemma*, St. Martins Griffin, 2020, 100), the average black twelfth grader reads at the same level as the average white eighth grader. That is not just a difference, it is an enormous difference. It is almost as though the two races are speaking two different languages. Some blacks complain the education difference is a result of tracking in school systems—in other words, tracking constitutes "systemic racism." They say white students are put on a fast track at an early age simply because they are white, while black students are put on a slow track, and therefore we need to get rid of tracking.

They miss the fact that tracking goes on at schools which are all-white. Tracking is done simply to help teachers do their job. If you put ten students who are good at reading into a class with ten students who are way behind in reading, the teacher can't teach both groups at once. One group will get bored and start shooting rubber bands while the teacher is working with the other group. Eliminating tracking is not the answer. The answer starts even before children reach school age; it starts with the family.

GENDER IDENTITY

In normal times, gender would be a topic subsumed under family, but these are not normal times. Nowadays people say things like, "I identify as trans," or "I identify as queer," and so forth—building their identity around a gender that is a human creation, not part of God's plan at all.

The more confused we are about gender, the better, in Satan's view. The more confused we are about gender, the greater will be the breakdown of the family structure ordained by God. And the greater the breakdown of the family, the further we will wander away from God and toward Satan's traps.

FAMILY IDENTITY

Yes, we build our identity by identifying with famous sports figures, or by identifying with leaders in all walks of life. And we build identity through personal achievements and comparing our achievements with achievements of others. But most of all we build our identity by identifying with our parents. Boys learn how to be men by watching their father; girls learn how to be women by watching their mother. Boys learn how to treat women by watching how their father treats their mother. Girls learn how to behave toward men by watching how their parents behave towards each other.

Building identity from our parents begins long before our first year of school. Some scientists believe it begins with the voices and music we hear even while in the womb. If our parents believe education is important, if they believe reading is important and they read books to us, those values will be transmitted to us. If our parents believe the values contained in God's laws—especially the Ten Commandments—are important, those values will be transmitted to us.

More than seventy percent of black children are born to unwed mothers. From day one, these unwed black parents are transmitting un-Godly values through their example to their children. From day one, one of the parents is not there to participate in child training, and the other parent is often absent earning a living. This situation cannot be blamed on systemic racism, because marriage licenses are equally available to blacks and whites. And this situation cannot be blamed on systemic racism, because black women are just as able as white women to say, "You have to marry me first."

The family structure in America is under attack. Our country is paying a steep price, but blacks are paying the steepest price of all. Our prisons are filled with black men raised without fathers. Black children are three and a half times as likely to be killed by abortion as white children, because the mothers know there will be no father to support them. Young black men are given a model of manhood that says school is for sissies, therefore drop out. Black men are assured that their problems are caused by racism—in other words, caused by someone else—therefore they have no responsibility. But God is just as strong to help, whether you are black or white. And God's laws about marriage apply whether you are black or white. There are no white men—or anyone else—preventing black men from taking marriage vows seriously, and there is no one preventing black women from insisting on marriage before children. As for systemic racism, there is nothing in the system telling black kids to drop out of school. They just have no fathers telling them "get back in school, kid, or else," and their mothers are too busy earning a living to help them with homework.

Critical race theory and the *1619 Project* do a lot to place blame for racism, but they offer no real solutions. The idea of reparations—some sort of financial payments from whites to blacks—is often mentioned; but what long-term value will that have? The long-term solution is to fix the black family structure according to God's laws: one wife, one husband, with the father taking responsibility as head of the family for seeing that the children are taught to obey God.

Adhering to a family structure based on God's laws does not mean black families will have no more problems, and it doesn't mean they will suddenly feel like they are no longer outsiders to a predominantly white society. But it does mean God will be with them, and God will support them in whatever trials they face. It means they can build a new identity as proud children of the Lord. "What then shall we say to this? If God is for us, who is against us?" (Romans 8:31).

AN IDENTITY OF RESPECT

We observed earlier: "Critical race theory says racism is an everyday experience for people of color." A black person may respond, "I don't need some fancy theory to tell me that!"

Say you're a black woman and you are in a store being helped by a white saleswoman. The saleswoman is dutifully showing you merchandise, but something about her demeanor has you saying to yourself, "I know what she is thinking ... she would rather not be helping me because I'm black." There is nothing overt in her behavior that you could take to court, but you sense something just the same. You leave the store feeling you experienced racism.

I have a surprise for you: You think this scene shows there is an unspoken gap between you and the white woman, but in fact it reveals something you have in common. The white woman knows from personal observation (if not from social statistics) that because you are a black woman the odds are strong that either you were born out of wedlock or you have borne children out of wedlock, or both. Her employer may have given her mandatory lectures on diversity and equity, but in her everyday life she "sees what goes on." She has something inside her, as a woman, which you have inside of you, as a woman: a knowledge that having children out of wedlock is wrong. It is something God has put inside you and inside her—a knowledge of right and wrong, a knowledge derived from the substance of Christ that God has put inside you both.

You will reply that the white woman was being judgmental. And you're right, she was being judgmental and she shouldn't be, "since all have sinned and fall short of the glory of God" (Romans 3:23). You may even guess she is a churchgoer, and decide (as some blacks have decided) that Christianity is a white man's religion and you want no part of it. That is not clear thinking. The subject of Christianity is Jesus Christ, not the saleswoman; and Jesus warned, "Not everyone who says to me, 'Lord, Lord,' shall enter the kingdom of heaven, but he who does the will of my Father who is in heaven" (Matthew 7:21).

Religious implications aside, the saleswoman's reaction reveals something blacks as a group must face. It shows that if black people want respect from others, they must demand respect of themselves. They can't pretend others don't "see what goes on," and they can't pretend God gives them a different moral compass because they are black. God gives everyone the same knowledge of right and wrong, and pointing the finger at white people for being racist does not excuse immorality. Pointing the finger at racist white people may create white guilt, but it will not bring respect. For blacks to obtain a position of higher respect in American society, the starting point cannot come from white people; the foundation lies in godly standards for black families.

The problems of different races may be different, but the solution is the same. The solution is to make the Ten Commandments the law of every home, black as well as white.

The solution is for the marriage covenant to be honored. The solution is for fathers to take their role seriously as head of the family and as enforcers of God's laws. The answer is to get all kids—especially inner city kids—out of public schools where they are taught there is no God, and where they are taught divisive teaching about racism, and into schools where God's laws will be honored and where the Ten Commandments will be on the wall. (How to accomplish this is a problem, but stating the case is at least a first step.) The answer is for us to pray that our kids will not be taught hatred, but will instead hear about God's love.

CHRISTIAN IDENTITY

When God led the people of Israel out of Egypt, out of the house of bondage, the first thing he did was give them his laws. He gave them the Ten Commandments and told them that just because they were free from the Egyptians did not mean they were free to do as they pleased. If they were to remain under God's protection, they would have to obey his commandments. For those people who turned to him, God made this promise:

> "Behold, at that time I will deal with all your oppressors. And I will save the lame and gather the outcast, and I will change their shame into praise and renown in all the earth" (Zephaniah 3:19).

God said, "I will deal with all your oppressors." In other words, if you really seek justice, turn first to God, not to man. God's word assures people of all races that he is in control of this world, as well as the next. We know that for those who serve God in truth and obedience, prayers of faith can move mountains. It is possible that the future of our country depends not on politicians, and not on billionaires, but on the faithfulness of a few humble believers—of all races—who seek God's favor in truth.

15
GENDER EQUALITY TEACHING SOWS CONFUSION

Disobedience Leads to Confusion

So, if God's word is being pushed aside, why doesn't God do something? We have documented in another chapter that God *is* doing something, though most people are not seeing it. [See message "God Speaks to America."] But God does not have to do anything dramatic for the effects of avoiding his word to be seen. God explained this to the prophet Jeremiah about 2600 years ago, when God's people were living in outright disobedience to God's commands. God said to Jeremiah, "Is it I whom they provoke? says the LORD. Is it not themselves, *to their own confusion?*" (Jeremiah 7:19 emphasis mine).

When we insist on challenging God's thinking, he gives us over to confusion. God doesn't have to *do* anything for confusion to set in. He is the Creator. He is the one who established a certain order. His commandments show us the way to live within that order. Therefore violation of his commandments leads to disorder, and disorder leads to confusion.

We have seen in the previous chapter how teachings about equality (and diversity-tolerance-inclusion) have brought confusion to families, especially black families. The idea of gender equality put forward by the women's liberation movement has been at the center of the confusion.

The Confusion of Women's Liberation

The women's liberation movement provides an example of confusion resulting from equality teaching. Women's liberation says men and women are equal, and we can forget God's plan for different roles of the sexes. Even many Christian women would agree. They would say God was right most of the time, but he was a little off in this case. It's time, the thinking goes, to have women in charge—women serving as generals in the army, women as police commissioners, women as corporate CEO's, and above all, wives as equal to husbands.

There is a sentence in the book of Genesis that must be repugnant to modern women's liberationists, and it may even be a sentence many Christian women wish to avoid. It is the sentence where God explains why he is creating woman. God had already created the first man, Adam, but when he saw Adam was alone, he said: "It is not good that the man should be alone; I will make him a helper fit for him" (Genesis 2:18). Then God took a rib from Adam and from that rib created woman to be Adam's helper. The liberationists scoff at the idea that a woman should be a helper to man. The idea goes counter to their crusade to prove a woman is an equal and a competitor to a man. But they can't avoid the fact that those words—"a helper fit for him"—are not the words of man, but the words of the God who created them, the God to whom they owe their life and breath. Isaiah warns those who try to overturn God's order of creation: "You turn things upside down! Shall the potter be regarded as the clay; that the thing made should say of its maker, 'He did not make me'; or the thing formed say of him who formed it, 'He has no understanding'?" And then he adds: "Woe to him who strives with his Maker, an earthen vessel with the potter!" (Isaiah 29:16; 45:9).

CONFUSION FOR MEN

Men are caught flat-footed by women's claims of equality. They may sense there is something wrong, but the American myth of equality, firmly implanted in their thinking, is inarguable to them. Schools have not taught them to check the Bible for alternative explanations. So men shut up, and privately scratch their heads, wondering what is going on.

What is going on is when women refuse to play their traditional role as wives and supporters—and this becomes the cultural norm—there is no role left for men. Because women are confused, men become confused. Men forfeit the leadership and protection roles they are supposed to be fulfilling. Some men end up saying, "Well, this is very nice not having to take on all that responsibility. I could get comfortable with this."

CONFUSION—AND ANGER—FOR WOMEN

Women's libbers mock at the old-fashioned labels of "ladies and gentlemen." Mixed audiences are now to be addressed simply as "guys." Liberated women remain adamant in their refusal to be "ladies" (with its implied dependency on men), but they complain loudly that men are not behaving as gentlemen. The complaints about men gradually grow into anger against men. And that's where we are today: equality leading to confusion, leading to frustration and anger.

God is in Control

And yet, through it all God himself is still in control. Today God answers as he answered his people in the time of Jeremiah. He said to his people, "How long will you waver, O faithless daughter? For the LORD has created a new thing on the earth: a woman protects a man" (Jeremiah 31:22).

We think we are in control. We think we are doing something very progressive. But God is in control. It is God who has created this new thing—"a woman protects a man"—in order to lead us into confusion. We don't stop to ask ourselves: If a woman protects a man, then who protects a woman? And so we end up with a #MeToo movement—a movement in which liberated, professional, supposedly independent women are all shouting in unison, "I need protection." Attempts to overturn God's plan lead to confusion—and then to frustration and anger because our plan is not working.

16
EQUALITY IN OUR SCHOOLS AND CHURCHES

Intellectual Honesty and
Martin Luther King, Jr.

Nowadays, school teachers who seek intellectual honesty have a tough job, as do Christian preachers. Americans pride themselves on their freedom of speech, but in spite of our boasted First Amendment rights, some things deemed to be critical of the principle of equality can't be said in public.

Consider, for example, the information presented earlier about Martin Luther King, Jr.—he cheated numerous times on his wife, attended orgiastic parties apparently without scruple, and plagiarized extensively in his doctoral thesis. When the Martin Luther King, Jr. holiday celebration rolls around, are school teachers going to mention these facts? Almost certainly not, since the principle of equality and the name of Martin Luther King, Jr. have become inextricably linked and enshrined as icons within the walls of academia.

What about a preacher on Sunday morning mentioning these facts about King? King's life would be an illustration of this passage from the second letter of Peter:

> "*They promise them freedom, but they themselves are slaves of corruption; for whatever overcomes a man, to that he is enslaved.* For if, after they have escaped the defilements of the world through the knowledge of our Lord and Savior Jesus Christ, they are again entangled in them and overpowered, the last state has become

worse for them than the first" (2 Peter 2:19–20 emphasis mine).

King's speeches offered people a promise of freedom, but he himself became overpowered by "the defilements of the world."

This could be a powerful lesson to people in the Christian community, but what are the chances of the story being told? Think about this: A white preacher preaching to a white congregation would be seen as fomenting racial hatred by saying such things about a black man. And a black preacher preaching to a black congregation would be resented for bursting a very big bubble. In both cases, they would probably end up saying, "What's the use? Better leave well enough alone." Equality, with Martin Luther King, Jr. as its figurehead, is firmly entrenched in our social consciousness. Any attempt to get rid of either one would upset too many people. Equality's shackles have reached firmly into both schools and churches.

I just referred to the principle of equality and the name of Martin Luther King, Jr., as "icons." Icon is another word for idol. Idols are condemned by the second of God's Ten Commandments. The preacher who says, "I guess I'd better leave well enough alone" should consider the implications: Has idol worship entered his church?

Gay Equality Reaches Schools and Churches

The gay lobby has latched onto equality as a powerful weapon to wield against Christian doctrine in both schools and churches. In public schools, the teaching of "marriage equality" has completely replaced God's teaching, and made the mention of Christian teaching forbidden. In churches this same language has prevailed partially, but not completely. Many liberal churches have completely caved, offering gay marriage ceremonies and ordination of gay ministers, while more conservative churches still hold the fort and adhere to biblical teaching that marriage is strictly between a man and a woman, and homosexuality is a sin.

So far, the infiltration of churches has happened in response to social pressure. But legal pressure on churches is on the horizon. Legislators in California have created a law making "conversion therapy" illegal. Conversion therapy is the gay lobby's pejorative term for any attempt of a Christian to tell a gay person Christ can save them from the gay lifestyle and from same-sex attraction. Part of the Christian gospel is to be outlawed in California—even in churches—in the name of equality.

A bill called the Equality Act has passed in the U.S. House of Representatives, but as of present writing has not passed in the Senate. If a future election should cause the composition of the Senate to change, however, the bill will no doubt be reintroduced. The Equality Act would add "sexual orientation" and "gender identity" (SOGI) as protected classes under the 1964 Civil Rights Act. It is hard to see how this act would give the LGBTQ lobby any more influence over public schools than they already have, but what about private Christian schools and churches? No doubt the LGBTQ will twist their conformity tourniquet as tight as they can to bring SOGI to everyone, everywhere.

Christians should be concerned, and should pray that the blood of Jesus would hold back the darkness which, in the name of equality, is coming across our country.

17
RESPONSIBILITY, NOT EQUALITY

The Tenth Commandment

While some people say equality made America a great country, I maintained earlier it was not equality that made our country great but opportunity. I want to amend that statement now. That statement is incomplete, because opportunity must be accompanied by responsibility. *Opportunity without responsibility is useless.* Responsibility comes from obedience to God's just decrees—decrees which proclaim, "Thou shalt" and "Thou shalt not"—commands which hold the individual responsible to the highest possible laws.

Modern equality teaching sows covetousness. By telling us, "Look at your neighbor, and if your neighbor has more of this thing or that thing than you have, then that is inequality, and you'd better demand your fair share." This idea violates God's tenth commandment which says, "You shall not covet … anything that is your neighbor's." (As pointed out earlier, the new word for demanding your fair share is equity. Equity is equality by subtraction, which means instead of keeping up with the Joneses by acquiring the same stuff the Joneses have, you take from the Joneses what they have. You bring them to your level.)

The tenth commandment is significant to everyone, not just to religious people. There are no federal or state or local laws that prohibit covetousness, but there are many—probably millions—of laws which deal with the *results* of covetousness. God's law gets to the root of the problem: one law instead of millions. By suppressing God's laws, our culture is multiplying problems for our people. People must be held responsible not just to a labyrinth of man-made laws, but for the covetousness which God's Spirit sees within our hearts.

The Only Answer is Christ

A Christian's first responsibility is obedience to Christ. Those who promote and teach equality seek to replace the mind of God (who created us unequal) with the mind of man (who declares, contrary to all evidence, that all men are created equal). The apostle Paul said, "'For who has known the mind of the Lord so as to instruct him?' *But we have the mind of Christ*" (1 Corinthians 2:16 emphasis mine). The mind of Christ must be our one and only source of truth. The solution is not to believe in some mythical equality, but to lay it all—our thoughts, our actions, our words—at the feet of Jesus Christ our Savior.

18
INTRODUCTION TO DIVERSITY, TOLERANCE, INCLUSIVENESS

Diversity, Tolerance, Inclusiveness Defined

Three words have become touchstones of modern American morality: diversity, tolerance, and inclusiveness. Taken at face value, these words have positive meanings.

My Webster's Collegiate Dictionary defines *diversity* as "the condition of being different: variety." When applied to people, this would mean something like "a variety of people" or "people who are different in lots of ways." When combined with *inclusiveness*, the implicit idea is all different people should include one another in their lives and activities. And *tolerance* means these people should be tolerant of one another's differences.

Together, these words draw a picture of general human camaraderie: different people all living together in an atmosphere of mutual tolerance. Who could argue with that? In application, however, the picture is different.

Diversity: In Practice

The *diversity* movement sees our population as divided into "minority groups" based on race (black, Hispanic, native American, etc.), sex (female), and gender identity (gay, lesbian, transgender, etc.). Every minority group is oppressed in some way. (The word minority carries no statistical meaning here since women are considered a minority even though numerically women are a majority of the population.) When all the minority groups are listed, the only people *not* on the list are white males. But any white male who is gay or transgender is also considered part of an LGBTQ minority group. According to these categories, therefore, all people except white, heterosexual males are part of some oppressed minority.

In the diversity lexicon, every minority group is suffering because it is under-represented in society—in government decision making, or in corporate boardrooms, or in athletic activities, or on the pay scale, etc. The additional implication is white, heterosexual males are over-represented, and therefore white, heterosexual males must have caused whatever grievances the minority group claims to suffer.

The logical result of this form of diversity is hatred of heterosexual white males. Hatred is not only the logical result, it is the *desired* result. It is desired because hatred forms the seeds of revolution, and revolution is the goal of the diversity people (see chapter on Black Lives Matter). Hatred for white, heterosexual males casts doubt on the validity of the U.S. Constitution. Pictures of the founding fathers of the American government show a group of white, heterosexual males working together to write our U.S. Constitution. The diversity movement concludes our government's foundations are corrupt and our Constitution should be discarded—an important idea for the revolution to take place.

Inclusiveness: In Practice

In practice, one common use of the idea of inclusiveness is to say all religions and philosophies (most recently the Muslim religion is singled out) are as acceptable as Christianity and should be welcomed (included) in our society. We'll talk more about religious inclusiveness later.

Aside from religious inclusiveness, the major emphasis on inclusiveness in America today comes from promoters of sexual immorality—most particularly from lobbyists for the LGBTQ (Lesbian-Gay-Bisexual-Transgender-Queer) community.

Inclusiveness is a favorite word of the LGBTQ. In 2017 the American women's soccer team elected to wear PRIDE jerseys with a rainbow motif in honor of the LGBTQ movement. When Joelene Hinkle (a Christian) declined to join the team because she did not want to wear an LGBTQ jersey, team member Ashlyn Harris tweeted, "Hinkle, our team is about inclusion." Harris further explained, "You would never fit into our pack or what this team stands for." The team's inclusiveness did *not* include Christian ideas of sexual morality.

When a twitter user pointed out that it looked like Christians were being targeted for exclusion, Harris was indignant. "Don't you dare say our team is 'not a welcoming place for Christians,'" Harris tweeted. "This is actually an insult to the Christians on our team. S[h]ame on you." Apparently other "Christians" on the team supported the LGBTQ cause and misrepresented their faith. They deserted the one person who held true to her faith, and they caused those outside the faith (like Harris) to misunderstand Christianity. They put a stumbling block in the way of someone outside the faith who might learn to honor the Lord, and they brought dishonor to one who truly honored the Lord.

How did this come about? Because the watchmen—their clergy—were asleep. Their watchmen were preaching what people wanted to hear. The shepherds were running at the sight of the wolf, leaving the flock to be gathered unknowingly into a pen marked for slaughter.

To return briefly to the subject of diversity: Anyone who has viewed a top-level soccer match knows there is a macho element associated with the sport. Soccer is a contact sport rewarding physical aggression and toughness and guile. Harris not only mimics men's aggression and toughness on the field, but she makes a point of dressing like a man off the field. When diversity women act and dress like men, are they increasing—or decreasing—diversity? This kind of diversity ends up robbing women of their womanhood, which God intended to be their true source of diversity.

Tolerance: In Practice

Even if you're not an engineer, you use the engineer's concept of tolerance when you shop for a new car. If you see wide gaps between the exterior panels on a car's body, you know instinctively that car is not well made. You realize the panels were fitted with a high tolerance for error. But panels that fit tightly together were assembled with a low tolerance, and you know the car is well made and will be long-lasting.

Today's moral climate is high tolerance—anything goes—and the tolerance level seems to get higher by the day. The moral "car" being constructed in American society will be poorly made and will soon cause a crash. God's laws, by contrast, are not even low tolerance. They are *zero* tolerance! God's laws are intended to make a vehicle that will last forever. While tolerance is a nice-sounding word, today's version of tolerance is the avowed enemy of Christian morality, and our society will eventually suffer the consequences.

Diversity, Tolerance, Inclusiveness Come as a Package

We have presented definitions of the three words standing separately. But in modern discourse, diversity, tolerance, and inclusiveness usually come as an implied package. When people use any of those words, they assume the other two words, as well. This collective definition causes confusion for a Christian when a diversity person quotes the Bible to support their version of morality. We should not be deceived, however. Though we may find elements of each piece of the diversity-tolerance-inclusiveness package appearing in Scripture, we need to know that the complete package they represent in today's culture is unscriptural.

For example, it might seem that Jesus should be applauded by diversity people for being inclusive when he ate with tax collectors and sinners. His ministry reached out to people of all different walks of life and different backgrounds. But by today's standards Jesus would *not* be called inclusive, because he characterized the tax collectors as sinners who needed to repent. He explained his actions by saying, "I have not come to call the righteous, but sinners to repentance" (Luke 5:32). Jesus did not add tolerance to his inclusive behavior, so he doesn't qualify as being inclusive in today's terminology. He was *intolerant* of any behavior that violated God's laws. He did not exhibit the full package of diversity-tolerance-inclusiveness. Jesus does not satisfy modern standards of American morality.

Here is a Christian perspective on the words diversity, tolerance, and inclusiveness:

The Lord God is the *author of diversity*. He made us all to be different for a purpose, and he did not create all people to be equal.

The Lord God is completely *inclusive*. The salvation he offers through his Son Jesus Christ is for all people everywhere, and he has commissioned his servants to spread the good news to the four corners of the earth.

The Lord God is completely *intolerant*. His law stands firmly fixed for all time. Jesus said, "Whoever then relaxes one of the least of these commandments and teaches men so, shall be called least in the kingdom of heaven; but he who does them and teaches them shall be called great in the kingdom of heaven" (Matthew 5:19). Even though we cannot meet God's zero-tolerance standards on our own, God has provided a way through the sacrifice of his Son on the cross. When we turn our lives over to Jesus Christ, his Holy Spirit will lead us in "paths of righteousness" (Psalm 23:3), and his righteousness will be imputed [credited] to us so we can stand before God's judgment seat.

19
HOW DIVERSITY-TOLERANCE-INCLUSIVENESS THINKING TWISTS THE WORDS OF THE BIBLE

The Modern Idea of Love

Psalm 78 describes the falling away of God's people from true teaching in this way: "they twisted like a deceitful bow" (Psalm 78:57). A twisted bow may look fine, but arrows shot from it will veer to the left or the right and miss their target.

Today we are seeing the biblical concept of love being twisted as though shot from a deceitful bow.

THE MODERN IDEA OF LOVE OPPOSES OBEDIENCE

Movies and videos give us the modern version of love: Love is feelings, and love is emotions deep inside us. Love is hormones that must be kept flowing. Love is an invisible fuel that gets poured into our emotional gas tank and makes us run fast. If we have our gas tank full of love, we have all that's needed. Steering the vehicle is unimportant. If love is there, who cares? I fill up my tank. You fill up your tank, and off we go. Whoopee!

God tells us we'd better follow the rules of the road or we will end up sorely disappointed. God warns us if we fill up the tank and step on the gas without following his rules, we'll smash into each other and cause a wreck. *Your love plus my love plus no steering wheels—that will not work.*

GOD'S LOVE REQUIRES OBEDIENCE

Christian love differs from Hollywood love because Christian love stresses the need for obedience. Obedience and Christian love are inextricably linked. Here are some of Jesus' statements to his disciples (with my emphasis added):

> "If you love me, you will *keep my commandments*" (John 14:15).

> "He who *has my commandments and keeps them*, he it is who loves me; and he who loves me will be loved by my Father, and I will love him and manifest myself to him" (John 14:21).

> "If a man loves me, he will *keep my word*, and my Father will love him, and we will come to him and make our home with him" (John 14:23).

> "He who does not love me does not *keep my words*; and the word which you hear is not mine but the Father's who sent me" (John 14:24).

> "If you *keep my commandments*, you will abide in my love, just as I have kept my Father's commandments and abide in his love" (John 15:10).

Jesus said it many times, so it would sink in: You cannot have Christian love separate from obedience. God gave us his laws and commandments *because he loves us*. By obeying his laws and commandments, we come under God's protection, and receive his love. And by obeying his laws and commandments, we return love to him.

The requirement for obedience in Christianity is referred to by the enemies of Christ as "hate speech." The LGBTQ community sees people as being hateful if they describe the LGBTQ lifestyle as sinful before God. LGBTQ defenders are shooting with a very twisted bow.

"Love Your Neighbor" is Not the First Commandment

Most Americans have probably heard the expression "love your neighbor as yourself," though they may not realize it comes from the Bible. Another related expression is "Do unto others as you would have them do unto you," which is a Ben Franklin paraphrase of Jesus' statement, "As you wish that men would do to you, do so to them" (Luke 6:31).

Even many Christians, however, may not remember "love your neighbor" was given by Jesus as the *second* commandment, not the first. Here is the complete passage:

> "And one of the scribes came up and heard them disputing with one another, and seeing that he answered them well, asked him, 'Which commandment is the first of all?' Jesus answered, 'The first is, Hear, O Israel: The Lord our God, the Lord is one; and you shall love the Lord your God with all your heart, and with all your soul, and with all your mind, and with all your strength. The second is this, You shall love your neighbor as yourself. There is no other commandment greater than these'" (Mark 12:28–31).

The one-two order of these commandments is not simply "giving God his credit," so to speak. The order is important because the ability to love our neighbor depends upon our love of God. According to the Bible, we cannot properly love our neighbor unless we first love the Lord our God. And we cannot love the Lord God unless we obey his commandments. The apostle John summarizes the idea in this concise statement:

> "By this we know that we love the children of God, when we love God and obey his commandments" (1 John 5:2).

The way to love our neighbor is to love God and to keep God's commandments. Disobedience to God's laws will ultimately bring disaster both to those who are disobedient, and to those who teach and approve of their disobedience. "Do unto others" can never be used as an argument to overturn God's moral laws (as today's homosexuals and lesbians try to do), or to deny God's role as Creator (as the transgender people try to do). "Do unto others" is never to be translated as, "If what you do does not make *me* feel *good*, then it cannot be loving." Biblical love is not measured by emotions.

"Judge Not"

Bible-believing Christians are often accused of being judgmental, with the Bible itself being used as ammunition against them. A Bible passage often quoted is Jesus' statement at Luke 6:37: "Judge not, and you will not be judged." Being judgmental is unloving. Those on the receiving end of the judging cry out, "Why don't you love your neighbor?" and "Why don't you do unto others as you would have them do unto you?" Their *feelings* tell them there is something wrong. Their sense of being judged has interrupted the free flow of all those emotions they depend on.

So what is a correct understanding of Jesus' statement about judging?

There are two functions performed by a judge. First, a judge decides whether a law has been broken, and if so, by whom. Second, a judge passes sentence on the guilty party. When Jesus said, "Judge not, and you will not be judged," he was speaking about the second function of the judge, the part where the judge passes sentence. Jesus' next words in the Bible passage are, "Condemn not, and you will not be condemned."

But modern thinking has taken "judge not" to refer to the first function of the judge, the function which determines whether a law has been broken. The modern emphasis on tolerance takes "judge not" to mean "do not judge someone else's behavior to be wrong or you may hurt their feelings."

Here are two examples from Jesus' ministry to illustrate the difference between the two kinds of judging, and to show what Jesus really meant.

First example: The scribes and the Pharisees murmured against Jesus and his disciples because they associated with sinners. The Pharisees asked Jesus, "'Why do you eat and drink with tax collectors and sinners?' But Jesus answered them, 'Those who are well have no need of a physician, but those who are sick; I have not come to call the righteous, but sinners to repentance'" (Luke 5:30–32). The modern non-judgmental, tolerance movement would have Jesus say something like, "They're not really sinners; they are all God's children." But Jesus *called* them sinners. He identified their behavior as contrary to God's laws. And he came to bring them God's mercy through repentance from their sinful behavior. Jesus judged their behavior as sinful, but he showed them a way to avoid the sentencing from the judge.

Second example: One morning Jesus was in the temple preaching, and the Pharisees presented a woman caught in adultery. They wanted to trap Jesus into saying something they could use against him before the authorities. They said, "Teacher, this woman has been caught in the act of adultery. Now in the law Moses commanded us to stone such. What do you say about her?" At first Jesus said nothing, but he bent over and began to write with his finger on the ground. As they continued to ask him, he stood up and said, "Let him who is without sin among you be the first to throw a stone at her." Then he bent over and continued to write with his finger on the ground. One by one, the Pharisees walked away, beginning with the oldest. Jesus looked up and said to the woman, "Woman, where are they? Has no one condemned you?" She said, "No one, Lord." And Jesus said, "Neither do I condemn you; go, and do not sin again" (John 8:3–11).

In this example, once again, the non-judgmental, tolerance people would have Jesus say to the woman, "You're fine just the way you are. Those Pharisees are just a bunch of nitpicking legalists." Instead, Jesus tells the woman she *is* a sinner, only he does not condemn her for her sin. He commands her not to sin again, which will demonstrate her repentance from her sin. *Jesus opposes the Pharisees—not for calling a sin a sin, but for not showing mercy to the sinner.*

20
TRUCKS IN THE ROAD

Disobedience is in Vogue

A widely accepted part of child rearing is encouraging a child to find himself, express himself, figure out what is true for him. Obedience has become an outdated concept, and sometimes disobedience is actually applauded. After all, how can a child (or adult) express himself if he is trying to adhere to someone else's rules?

Any mother, however, who saw her child run out into a busy street to fetch a ball, would immediately grab that child out of the way of oncoming traffic. It would not occur to her to say, "Johnny is expressing himself now" when a big truck was roaring down on him. The shaken mother would say to Johnny, "Always remember to look to the right and to the left before entering the street."

This picture of the child running into the street is analogous to what is going on in America's spiritual life right now. Most people don't read the Bible. And if they read it, they don't believe it. The Bible—and Christians who believe in the Bible—would tell them to look to the right and the left, because there are trucks in the road. But they say, "What trucks? I don't see any trucks. You're making that up in an attempt to upset me and impose your rules on me. I choose to live by my own rules, thank you very much."

SPIRITUAL "TRUCKS" AROUND US

There are unseen spiritual "trucks" all around us—demonic forces stirred up into constant activity by their sovereign ruler, Satan. One purpose of God's word is to help us defend against and defeat these spiritual forces, even though we cannot see them. God's word makes us aware of the human activities Satan can use to bring demonic forces into our lives. Many of these activities were described in Part I of this book.

Some readers, especially older readers, may say I am exaggerating or imagining when I talk so much about demons. But there are things becoming common now which were not common a generation ago. Keep a watch out for the man whose mind is not under his control, but is controlled by something that glows like small, hot coals behind his eyes. Keep a watch out for the woman who stares ahead without comprehension while angry words flood unrestrained from her mouth. Watch, and I think you will begin to see.

Isaiah 60:18 tells us, "You shall call your walls Salvation, and your gates Praise." It is important to have both the walls of salvation and the gates of praise. Obedience to God's laws provides the walls, that is, God's protection from the dangerous spiritual traffic. We obey God's road signs in order to avoid Satan's demonic trucks. And while we follow the road signs, we are also praising God. The gates (of praise) control what thoughts enter and leave our minds. We are not walking along the road in fear, but in a spirit of rejoicing. Not only has God given us good safety instructions, but he is actually walking with us, giving us his comfort and security every step of the way. Entering by gates of praise allows us to live "in Christ" (John 15:4).

Prayer Makes a Difference

The prayers of Christians invoke God's protection upon our society—which means protection of atheists as well as believers. We know that our Lord is "a God merciful and gracious, slow to anger and abounding in steadfast love and faithfulness" (Psalm 86:15).

In the Bible, the patriarch Abraham gives us an example of how the prayer of one person can protect an entire society. Abraham pleaded with God to hold back the destruction God had planned for the wicked city of Sodom. Abraham knew God might bring punishment to Sodom for its great sins, but Abraham also knew his righteous nephew Lot and Lot's family lived there. So Abraham asked: If God could find just ten righteous people left in Sodom, would God please hold back his punishment? And God answered Abraham's prayer, and said, "For the sake of ten I will not destroy it" (Genesis 18:32).

Similarly, today God shows mercy to a land for the sake of the prayers of a few believers—for the sake even of ten. Only prayers in the powerful name of Jesus are able to restrain the speeding trucks—the demonic powers—Satan constantly aims at us. There is no other power, in any religion or philosophy, capable of stopping or casting out demons.

21
GUIDING PRINCIPLES AT
AMERICAN UNIVERSITIES

The Principle of Classical Inclusiveness

American universities are pacesetters for the country's moral culture.

Changes in our universities' culture have been occurring for a long time. The first colleges in the country were established to train Christian ministers. Those schools (think Harvard, Yale, and Princeton) gradually became secularized over centuries. The changes took place in a consistent direction: namely, toward a classical education in the humanities and sciences—with religion still taught, but taught as an alternate subject rather than as an absolute basis of faith. I call this direction of change "classical inclusiveness."

Classical inclusiveness means a university presents itself as a kind of buffet table of great philosophers, great artists, and great thinkers from all fields. There is general agreement about who those great thinkers are (Plato, Aristotle, Shakespeare, Darwin, etc., etc.), and general agreement that a well-educated person will profit from learning about these thinkers, but will remain free to come to his own decisions about what he believes to be true. He can fill his plate with intellectual goodies as his tastes dictate.

The effect of this buffet table approach is for the university to place the Bible and Christianity on the same level as any other religion or philosophy—that is, on the second level down, not the top. At the top level is the principle of inclusiveness itself, plus the individual's powers of judgment and rationalization.

The Principle of Identity Politics

Classical inclusiveness can still be found as a part of the curriculum, at least at most universities. But beginning a few decades ago, a new principle entered the scene: the principle of identity politics. In this new era of education, a certain *identity* is placed at the top of the scholastic pyramid, with the identity being the identity of gender or race, or sometimes both combined. All of history and literature—and even science—is now to be seen through the prism of gender or racial identity. Students are required to critique any piece of art or literature or music and explain how the identity of the author warped the author's view and how a different gender or racial identity would have provided a correct view. Entirely new departments of study have sprung up, devoting themselves to interpreting the world from a feminist point of view, or from a racial point of view, or from the view of some other perceived minority.

More About Equity: The Principle of Let's Get Even

This principle of identity politics has become firmly entrenched at most universities over a period of several decades—a relatively short time. But in recent years it has given birth to another principle, which I call the "let's get even" principle—a principle which in the media has been given the misleading name "equity."

The phrase "to get even" has a double meaning. The literal meaning aligns it with the American ideal of equality. It echoes the ideal of "all men are created equal" and implies if there is any way in which we observe men *not* to be equal, then it is the fault of society, and we should take steps to *fix* society. We should bring about a situation in which all people are *even* with each other.

The second meaning of "getting even" is paying someone back for a perceived slight. This idea harbors the vindictiveness implied in the statement, "I'll get even with you, you so-and-so." It's the false justice of the street gang that says, "Let's loot that store because they charge too much. And remember how the manager called the police when he caught one of our members shoplifting, so we need to get even with him."

Sadly, this second meaning has ascended to the top of the pyramid in academic thinking. If identity politics reveal some inequality in race or gender, then somebody must be blamed and gotten even with. The street gang mentality has been accorded the status of a principle of justice in the eyes of

261

academic authorities. If a group stages a protest, saying they have suffered from some sort of unequal treatment (including any imagined verbal microaggression), then the university authorities must obsequiously apologize to them and promise to do better next time. Alas, one way the authorities have found to do better is to lower academic standards. If people of certain minority groups can gain entrance to university with lower test scores than other groups, they will get even in both senses of the phrase. Feminists and homosexuals get academic credit by writing scholarly-sounding papers to prove Jesus would approve of gay marriage, or to show the command to "love your neighbor" justifies all sorts of sexual deviance. In these ways, they will *get even* with those hateful Christian fundamentalists. And so forth.

In a previous chapter I defined equity as "equality by sub-traction." Now I am amplifying that to read "subtraction with attitude," or "subtraction with a vengeance." During Communist China's Cultural Revolution this same concept of equity prevailed. University professors were sent to work as field laborers to "teach them a lesson." Those who objected, or even looked like they might object, were executed.

The *get even* mentality has quickly spiraled out of control in America and turned into hatred and violence. We see it happening on campuses and on city streets across the country. How could this happen? How can teaching about nice-sounding things like equality and diversity and inclusiveness descend into hatred? It happens because God's laws are ignored. God's salvation is deemed unneeded, and the love of God in Christ Jesus our Lord is nowhere to be found.

"Let's Get Even" has a Crucial Difference from Left-Wing Ideologies

Even when classical inclusiveness led universities to promote left-wing ideologies, they still made a pretense of scholarship—studying the writings of Karl Marx or Bertrand Russell or whoever, and writing reports based on what was written. And even the identity-focused studies departments have made a pretense of scholarship—studying the writings of some historical figure and reporting their identity-centered interpretation of what was written. But the *let's get even* (equity) movement is based on feelings—feelings of being oppressed, feelings that justify themselves in resistance to any logical argument. There is no scholarship involved at all—no need to examine data or facts.

Recently a TV reporter investigated the fate of billions of dollars of federal aid which had been sent to a certain city. The funds did not seem to have had any effect on conditions in that city. He invited a city councilman to appear on his program, but when he asked the city councilman about the funds, the councilman replied, "I'm not here to talk about the money. I'm here to talk about 400 years of institutional racism." And every question the reporter asked the councilman resulted in the same answer: He kept repeating it all boils down to 400 years of racism. His feelings of oppression were more important than investigating facts and figures.

The councilman's attitude reflects what is happening in academia and is now dominating the public forum. Supporting one's accusations with facts and analysis is considered beside the point. The feelings of the oppressed minorities—the expressions of grievances, whether real or imagined—are most important. Satan loves this situation because now he can whisper messages of hate into his subjects' ears and feel confident they will not be diverted by rational arguments.

22
UNEXPECTED (?) RESULTS AT UNIVERSITIES

Lack of Authority at Universities

What university authorities apparently don't understand is their pathetic lack of authority is the outcome of their own teaching. When students have visited the buffet table of classical thinkers, educators have told them (sometimes with deliberate subversion in mind) to browse freely and not be constrained by any rigid traditions or morality—to think for themselves and question authority.

Whether they realize it or not, universities have undermined their own claim to authority. America's prestigious universities long ago abandoned the authority of the Bible and the Christian God. Returning to God's authority never even occurs to them as an option.

Christian parents, beware: When you send your children off to college, their brave new world will be a world of no authority, including parental authority.

"Return to Classics" Poses Dangers

Some American Christians align themselves with secular conservatives who call for a return to the teaching of the classics. They would like to see a return to classical inclusiveness, the buffet table of great ideas. In part this is because the "great ideas of history" are associated with the men who wrote the U.S. Constitution, which in turn has provided Americans with an amazingly stable government and religious protection. Our Constitution is a heritage worth preserving, and Christians and others are rightfully concerned that young people will grow up without learning to appreciate and preserve this heritage.

But the buffet table of great ideas also poses dangers. It reduces Christianity to one of many ideas, with the mind of the student as sole arbiter of what is true and what is not true. Christian students will be warned against regarding Christianity as containing *exclusive* truth. Finding *some* truth in Christianity is okay, but saying there is no way to truth except through Christ will (they maintain) inhibit open dialogue.

An example of this mindset is found at the Yale Center for Faith and Culture established by the Yale Divinity School. The center offers a course for undergraduates which presents works of various philosophers and thinkers, as well as religious texts, so the student can do comparison shopping. The advertised goal of the course is to allow students to find for themselves the ideas that will allow them to live a "good life." Not a *Christian* life, but a *good* life. The starting assumption is the mind of the teenage student can fully decide what constitutes a "good life."

The Stumbling Block of Human Wisdom

I once heard a preacher say, "The worst form of badness is human goodness." His point was that when we try to establish our own "human goodness," it leads us away from the need for repentance. It leads us away from the need for Christ's salvation.

I would like to propose a paraphrase of that preacher's statement directed specifically to our university culture. My paraphrase would be: The worst form of ignorance is human wisdom. Christians—especially Christian college students—need to be aware that academic pride is always trying to side-step Christ's claim to be the sole source of truth. "'I am the way, *and the truth*, and the life,' Jesus said; 'no one comes to the Father, but by me'" (John 14:6, emphasis mine). And the apostle Paul said, "The wisdom of this world is folly with God" (1 Corinthians 3:19). Academic achievement convinces us we can find truth and goodness through our magnificent brain power. But our brains can't fix our hearts. Only Christ can do that. And true wisdom begins with God's Spirit in our heart.

Inclusiveness Fails to Help Achieve Diversity

Universities today are in competition to see who can claim the greatest diversity on campus. This means attracting students from a variety of cultures and backgrounds and geographical locations. Mixing all these different groups together could result in friction between the groups, but academia has decided to rely on the religion of inclusiveness to come to the rescue.

Once people understand inclusiveness, the thinking goes, they will all get along with each other. By preaching the new religion of inclusiveness, the university can say in effect, "Everyone continue with your private set of values, as long as your highest value remains inclusiveness. Then there will be no more conflict and everyone on campus will be happy. And when you graduate and go out into the world with this new value system of inclusiveness, then everyone in the world will learn from you how to get along, and there will be no more wars."

Sure enough, many are graduating into the adult world and raising high the banner of inclusiveness. However, conflicts do not seem to go away.

Inclusiveness and Moral Values are Mutually Exclusive

So why is there so much conflict and discontent on *inclusive* college campuses? Instead of resting comfortably in a warm cocoon of inclusiveness, students become confused, then embittered and resentful.

There are two problems with trying to live by the rule of inclusiveness.

The first problem concerns moral values. We make choices in life, and since we are human beings, we make our choices based on our personal values. As soon as my values differ from my neighbor's values, some conflict is inevitable. Values declare some things to be of high value, and other things to be of lower value or of negative value. Values are exclusive. As soon as we establish personal moral values, inclusiveness goes out the door.

INCLUSIVENESS REMOVES GOD FROM THE MORAL EQUATION

The second and more fundamental problem with inclusiveness is it sets itself above God's laws. It attempts to make God's laws subordinate to a philosophical principle. No amount of philosophical or moral debate can remove God from his position as supreme Ruler over all, and God's laws are absolute and exclusive. Jesus said, "For truly, I say to you, till heaven and earth pass away, not an iota, not a dot, will pass from the law until all is accomplished" (Matthew 5:18).

INCLUSIVENESS RESORTS TO COMPROMISE

When inclusiveness encounters conflict, it resorts to compromise. Inclusiveness blurs lines of division. Inclusiveness has few hard barriers, while emphasizing the importance of all points of view.

A university campus ministry invited a doctoral student in theology to speak to a group of undergraduates. The speaker admonished the Christian students never to speak in an exclusive way when discussing their religion with people of other faiths. To do so might offend the listeners and would not promote open discussions, he maintained. Set inclusiveness as your highest value, and keep everyone happy. The ordained ministers who organized the event were in complete agreement with the speaker.

But what the speaker recommended is intellectual dishonesty. Christianity makes exclusive claims (as do most other religions). Jesus said, "I am the way, and the truth, and the life; no one comes to the Father, but by me" (John 14:6). Jesus our Savior shed his blood for those exclusive claims. Many Christian martyrs have shed their blood for those exclusive claims. If we cancel those claims, we are not being true to our faith—we are denying our Savior.

Compromise has consequences. When Satan's trucks come roaring down the road, they will plow effortlessly through any scholarly roadblocks which compromise or dilute the Christian Gospel.

23
DIVERSITY, TOLERANCE, INCLUSIVENESS IN COMMERCE

Thought Control in American Business

Did your mother ever tell you, "If you can't say something nice about someone, then don't say anything at all?" Good advice for getting along in society. Control your tongue, regardless of the thoughts going through your mind. But in the world of diversity-tolerance-inclusiveness there is something new afoot: You are required to police your mind and your thinking—not just your tongue. You are required to be "woke."

American business executives take the lead in this effort. Midsize and large companies now have a diversity czar, along with mandatory diversity education classes for employees. You cannot be employed by American big business without receiving an education in diversity-tolerance-inclusiveness. This is a phenomenon that deserves much more attention by Christians, because it is possible to get a failing grade and be out of a job. Are Christians on the way to being squeezed out of the job market?

AN EXAMPLE: AIRBNB

Airbnb is a company that connects travelers with host families who allow the travelers to stay in their home for a fee. The billionaire CEO of Airbnb, Brian Chesky, has placed the following statement on the Airbnb website:

> At the heart of our mission is the idea that
> people are fundamentally good, and every

community is a place where you can belong. I sincerely believe that [discrimination] is the greatest challenge we face as a company.[3]

This is a simplistic statement of religious belief, with theological implications. The statement says "people are fundamentally good," which dispenses with the Christian doctrine of original sin. And by dispensing with sin, the statement removes the need for salvation from sin, and thus the need for a Savior. What sounds at first like a simple, maybe even innocent, statement of belief, is a repudiation of Christian belief. But that is just the beginning.

A Christian writer posted an article (Marvin Olasky, *World Magazine*, February 4, 2017) about his experience with Airbnb, in which he showed the results of such a seemingly innocent statement of beliefs. He and his wife acted as Airbnb hosts over a period and became recognized as "Superhosts," meaning they got uniformly positive reviews from their many guests. Then they received a notice from Airbnb that all hosts would now have to sign the following Airbnb agreement:

> I agree to treat everyone in the Airbnb community—regardless of their race, religion, national origin, ethnicity, disability, sex, gender identity, sexual orientation, or age—with respect, and without judgment or bias.

Those last four words caught his attention: "without judgment or bias." If you want to work for Airbnb, it's not sufficient to control your tongue; you must now control your thoughts, and get rid of any judgmental thoughts.

---

3   [copied from www.airbnb.com/diversity in June, 2018]

Technically, no human being could with honesty sign the Airbnb agreement. As human beings, we make decisions based on our personal set of values. By definition, personal values place religion, philosophy, age, ethical behavior, etc. in a certain hierarchy. Values claim certain things are *better* than others. To pretend we have no set of values (and therefore never exercise judgment) is to pretend not to be human. And to pretend we consider the next person's set of values to be of equal value to our set of values would be verbal nonsense—causing the word "value" to be of no value.

The threat behind the Airbnb agreement soon became clear. The author of the article refused to sign the agreement, and Airbnb promptly canceled his account and all his future reservations. Furthermore, he was no longer permitted to make reservations for himself as a guest with other Airbnb hosts. Airbnb did not, as it turned out, consider *all* people to be "fundamentally good." Airbnb had a certain set of values which they were determined to enforce with judgmental fervor and unapologetic bias. What is their set of values? The fact that they give special regard to a person's "sex, gender identity, sexual orientation" is a strong clue: Their values are aligned with the LGBTQ lobby and against Bible-based Christianity. They are woke, and everyone they employ must be equally woke.

MORE EXAMPLES

Airbnb is just one example. Watch the news and see how many CEOs of major companies speak out in lockstep with the LGBTQ lobby to protest any legislation opposed by that lobby. The LGBTQ lobby has a strong "diversity presence" in the boardrooms of big business in America, and through those boardrooms they are influencing government legislative decisions. Big business operates in mortal fear of the woke crowd. It's be woke or go broke.

Most of us have read the news stories of small business people like bakers and florists being taken to court because they refuse to provide their services for a gay wedding. If we are Christian believers, we may feel sympathetic toward these people, but we see them as outliers—extreme examples of a problem not likely to reach most of us. And as for Airbnb, most people will not have their income solely dependent on profits from Airbnb, so that case doesn't threaten most of us personally.

But Christians need to open their eyes. Consider this situation: A Christian man is a middle manager at Big Corp USA and has three years remaining until retirement. He receives a notice stating all managers will now be required to train their employees in diversity. They must train employees to remove (you guessed it) all "judgment or bias" in their relationships with other employees, regardless of any sexual deviance by the employee—a deviance which God himself calls (with "judgment and bias") an abomination. The manager is at an age when it would be difficult to find a similar job at another company. Plus, he is aware other companies in the same industry are making the same requirements of their managers. He has a family to support. It's a tough situation for a person who takes his Christian faith seriously.

Christians beware: These new values, professing to include everybody, are aimed at excluding you.

A Spiritual Beast

There is a passage in the Book of Revelation which has been the subject of much speculation. In this passage, the apostle John is recording a prophecy he received from Jesus, and he describes a beast (a spiritual beast) which will rise out of the earth:

> "… it [the beast] causes all, both small and great, both rich and poor, both free and slave, to be marked on the right hand or the forehead, so that no one can buy or sell unless he has the mark, that is, the name of the beast or the number of its name" (Revelation 13:16–17).

Various suggestions have been offered about what the "mark of the beast" might be. Some say it will be a computer chip hidden under the skin or some sort of permanent tattoo. But the mark in the vision is a symbolic mark, it is not a physical mark. The forehead is symbolic of a person's mind—the way a person thinks—and the right hand is symbolic of a person's ability to work. *People will be required to think a certain way in order to conduct business. People must be woke to hold a job.* The mark of the beast in America today is a person's allegiance to diversity-tolerance-inclusiveness ideas—ideas which require that our judgment of right and wrong differ from God's standards. It will soon be true that "no one can buy or sell unless he has the mark"—the mark of correct thinking, the mark of diversity-tolerance-inclusiveness thinking.

The Beast Takes Control

The author has witnessed firsthand the power of the beast. Business leaders capitulate to the beast, not because they believe diversity-tolerance-inclusiveness principles will result in a better corporate product, but out of fear. They eagerly welcome the beast through their corporate front door—to insure the beast does not trample their company underfoot. They welcome the beast to insure the Human Rights Campaign does not alert the media to their lack of wokeness. They welcome the beast so the Southern Poverty Law Center does not add them to their list of haters. They welcome the beast so the ACLU will have no reason to bring them to court. They welcome the beast so they can continue to receive government contracts from woke government agencies. They compete to show a bigger welcome to the beast than the next guy, to insure that they win the contract.

The beast truly behaves like a beast.

What is at Stake Here?

In Revelation chapter 18 Jesus describes how in a single hour the great city of Babylon—a city used to symbolically represent human depravity and sexual immorality—will be destroyed. Jesus prophesies that in that hour "the merchants of the earth weep and mourn for her [Babylon], since no one buys their cargo any more, cargo of gold, silver ..." (Revelation 18:11-12), and he gives a long list of all the items that brought wealth to the merchants of the earth. The final item on the list is "human souls."

You might ask, "Is that really what is at stake here—human souls? Isn't that a bit of an exaggeration?" It is not an exaggeration. The beast will have his fill. Wokeness represents a rebellion against God's life-giving word. The religion of diversity-tolerance-inclusiveness is a spiritual deathtrap.

THE ONE AND ONLY SOLUTION

When the apostle Paul visited Athens, he encountered a city that had no knowledge of God and worshiped pagan idols. Acts chapter 17 records a speech Paul made to the men of Athens, in which he proclaimed the truth about the one true God. The last sentence of his speech begins with these words: "The times of ignorance God overlooked" (Acts 17:30). The phrase "times of ignorance" means the times when there was no knowledge of the true God and of his offer of salvation through Jesus Christ. Paul's speech could be paraphrased this way: "But now there is no ignorance. *Now there is no excuse.* The knowledge of Jesus Christ is here for everyone, and it is that knowledge which I proclaim to you today."

Then Paul said, "But now he [God] commands all people everywhere to repent." This is not a suggestion from God, it is a command. It is a requirement, affecting both thinking and behavior. Repentance means a change of mind and a change in behavior, a determination to obey all of God's laws. The command affects "all people everywhere." No one is exempt.

Next, Paul said there is an urgent reason for repentance: "because he [God] has fixed a day on which he will judge the world in righteousness by a man whom he has appointed" (Acts 17:31). Life will go on and on, day after day, with everything seeming the same and with most people going about their activities oblivious to what is coming. But on a single day, God will judge the entire world. He will judge the world according to the words and commands of his Son Jesus Christ. And his judgment will determine the eternal fate of each human soul.

In case anyone wants to question these facts, God has given an absolute guarantee through Jesus' resurrection from the dead. "And of this he has given assurance to all by raising him from the dead" (Acts 17:31). In that one speech, Paul summarized the human situation in a nutshell.

Merchants get rich by selling human souls. Christians are challenged to say, "My soul is not for sale."

24
DIVERSITY, TOLERANCE, INCLUSIVENESS, AND THE LGBTQ LOBBY

The LGBTQ Lobby Attacks Biblical Christianity

Of all the groups staking out territory in the inclusiveness domain, the LGBTQ community has claimed the most. This group has given inclusiveness a set of iron teeth and achieved the improbable result of making inclusiveness exclusive.

The LGBTQ proponents make a conscious and direct attack on biblical Christianity. Christians need to be fully aware.

The purported purpose of inclusiveness seems to allow different groups of people to be who they are—and to get along with each other. Theoretically Christians are allowed to be Christians, and gays, lesbians and transgender people are allowed to be what they want to be. Everyone should get along with each other.

The reality is different. The LGBTQ lobby has used the equality card to claim a right for men to marry men and women to marry women. This is supposed to allow them to feel included in society. And they demand that everyone honor their right to marry in this way. "Everyone" includes Christian ministers, Christian charities, Christian businesses, Christian politicians, and so forth. And LGBTQ values must be taught in all schools, to children of all religions. The Christian belief in marriage as a sacred sacrament between a man and a woman is nullified by law. The Christian teaching that homosexuality is an abomination to God is reversed by law, and the new teaching is force-fed to our children. And, by and large, Americans are saying, "Okay, why not?"

The reason why not is it means our society as a whole is shaking a fist at God and saying, "I don't care about your laws, God, and I don't believe you can to do anything about it, either. You can go jump in the lake." But God will not jump in the lake. He sits on his throne in heaven and see everything.

God Himself Co-opted by the LGBTQ Movement

Ironically, LGBTQ people often look for inclusion within the general framework of the Christian religion. Some don't want to abandon the Christian heritage. Gays and lesbians can be heard to say, "God made me this way. That God you talk about so self-righteously—the fact that I'm gay or lesbian is his doing. If you are right, then God must be breaking his own laws."

But God does not break his own laws. Christians who know the Bible know homosexuality is an abomination to God. God said so repeatedly in both the Old and New Testaments. And they know God does not create anyone homosexual. There is no homosexual gene, no genetic cause for homosexuality. The most dedicated pro-LGBTQ researchers have not been able to find such evidence. And there is no biological cause of transgender desires—quite the opposite. Christians see that homosexual and transgender behavior arise from a spirit of disobedience, not from biological causes. God does not break his own laws. Homosexuality has spiritual, not genetic, roots.

The LGBTQ lobby works hard to suppress these facts, and it works doubly hard at painting conservative Christians as haters. The LGBTQ efforts to change public thinking have been effective. The iron teeth of inclusiveness are succeeding in suppressing the voices of Christians. The iron teeth of inclusiveness are succeeding in crushing any public opposition to LGBTQ causes and even convincing people God himself is woke.

But God sees and God will act. God can't be co-opted by anybody. Christians who issue warnings about breaking God's laws are not haters but are performing a service—a service similar to that of the weatherman who predicts a storm. As I have documented in a previous chapter ("God Speaks to America"), God sees, and God takes action. Christians in America who are afraid to speak up will be affected as much as atheists.

The LGBTQ Lobby Condemns "Conversion Therapy"

LGBTQ activists have coined the term "conversion therapy" to describe any Christian attempts to convince gays they don't have to be gay, and that they would be happier if they obeyed God's laws. The LGBTQ activists strongly condemn such efforts as hateful and as causing guilt and anxiety in gays. They claim conversion therapy leads to depression and even suicide. They have convinced mainstream health organizations to denounce conversion therapy, and they have persuaded legislators in some areas to pass laws prohibiting it.

But the term "conversion therapy" is misleading. Jesus was not a therapist. Jesus never said, "Come back to see me again next week with a check for $100, and we'll talk about this some more." Jesus spoke a word, and a person was changed forever.

And healing by the power of Jesus still happens. When Jesus speaks, a person is changed forever. The LGBTQ lobby (along with many supporters) may deny this is possible, but it *is* possible, and change happens—though there is no human prescription for making it happen. In the time of Jesus' ministry, change did not happen to everyone. There were many unbelievers, and many without faith. And the same is true today. Some will receive Jesus, and some will not. There is no cookbook procedure, no set of rules to write in a medical textbook.

What Christians preach is not therapy. What Christians preach is "Christ crucified, a stumbling block to Jews and folly to Gentiles, but to those who are called, both Jews and Greeks, *Christ the power of God and the wisdom of God*" (1 Corinthians 1:23–24 emphasis mine).

Hope and Promise for All LGBTQ Persons

God gives a strong encouragement to any LGBTQ participant who senses something has gone wrong. If you are gay, know there *is* a way out. Jesus Christ himself is the way. He is the *only* way. He is "the way, and the truth, and the life" (John 14:6). Jesus is alive today, and he has the power to bring you out of the gay lifestyle. He has the power to give you a new life, holy and pure in the eyes of God—a life in which God's love replaces all anxiety and fear.

IT ISN'T EASY

Jesus holds out his hand to every LGBTQ person, pleading with him or her to accept Christ and be transformed by Christ's resurrection power. But transformation doesn't mean Christianity offers an EASY button. A person may be dramatically changed by Christ, but the road ahead won't be easy. The Christian life is never easy, regardless of a person's starting point. Jesus warned "the gate is narrow and the way is hard, that leads to life, and those who find it are few" (Matthew 7:14). The new Christian will experience a peace that passes all understanding—a peace he or she never experienced in life as an LGBTQ person. But the demons who had a comfortable home in that person for so long will clamor at the door, trying to get back in. Satan will urge those demons on, exhorting them to break down the door and lure a person back to the LGBTQ lifestyle.

And jealous onlookers in the LGBTQ community will bay like hounds after the new convert, saying, "Don't let Christ have a victory. Come back and join with us, your old friends. Don't be fooled by conversion therapy stuff." They can't bear to see someone who was once like them gaining a new life of freedom. Yet Jesus gives all believers this assurance: "He who endures to the end will be saved" (Matthew 24:13).

How the LGBTQ Movement Deals with Guilt

The LGBTQ lobby opposes conversion therapy because they claim conversion therapy causes guilt, which leads to anxiety. But there is a serious problem with their logic. *The root cause of guilt is not therapy, but sin.* They propose to get rid of guilt by simply re-defining sin—by telling everyone what society used to consider sin is no longer sin. What used to be excluded behavior is now included, simply by their redefinition. The assumption is that guilt is created by man, by man-made laws, and therefore man is free to say, "I've washed my hands. There is no sin. I am not guilty."

But there is only one way to remove guilt—through Jesus Christ. There are no loopholes. There is no redefining of sin. God said simply, "For I the LORD do not change" (Malachi 3:6). We all stand before God as sinners. Without Christ, there will always be anxiety, because human declarations of innocence cannot remove guilt.

GUILT IN THE BATHROOM MIRROR

LGBTQ people may think a majority vote by society will eliminate their guilt, but their bodies will always bear witness to them that there is something deeply wrong. The pieces in their anatomical jigsaw puzzle don't fit together right. The picture they form doesn't match the puzzle's box cover and is perverted and distorted. Guilt will always be staring at them in the bathroom mirror, and there will always be anxiety.

Why do they call their parades and their public events "PRIDE" events? Externally, they are declaring their public defiance against old-fashioned definitions of sin, telling the world they are free to define sin in their own way, and telling Christians if you don't like it, you can lump it.

Internally they cover up anxiety and guilt with a boastful show, suppressing what they know inside themselves to be true. They rely on the sheer force of verbal repetition to wipe away the picture they face in the mirror every morning.

It won't work. Only the power of God, released through the sacrificial blood of Jesus Christ, can save them. The expression "Jesus saves" is true. Jesus has the power to forgive sins, and the power to overcome all causes of sin, in all of us—including the spirit of disobedience at the root of homosexual desires.

LGBTQ people think Christianity condemns them, and they are 100% right. Christianity condemns all of us. We all stand as sinners before a holy and righteous God. Only the grace of God, released through the sacrificial blood of Jesus Christ, can save any of us. The apostle Paul said, "Wretched man that I am! Who will deliver me from this body of death? Thanks be to God through Jesus Christ our Lord!" (Romans 7:24–25).

Victory for the Human Rights Campaign

The integrity of America's medical establishment is guarded by a number of professional organizations, including the American Medical Association, the American Association for Marriage and Family Therapy, the American Psychological Association, and others. These organizations strive to maintain high standards of medical treatment based on clinical data, but they are not immune to political pressure.

The Human Rights Campaign (HRC) is a powerful organization in Washington, D.C., whose sole purpose is to champion LGBTQ causes. Under pressure from the HRC, our leading medical organizations have made solemn pronouncements that gay, lesbian, and transgender behavior is normal, and conversion therapy is harmful. These official statements are like gold bullion to the LGBTQ lobby. LGBTQ people are now officially—medically, scientifically—declared normal, based on documents from professional organizations. Anyone who declares otherwise must be motivated (they say) by prejudice and hatred. And anyone who performs conversion therapy can be sued in a court of law in some jurisdictions.

The LGBTQ people feel vindicated, and the professional organizations are relieved to get rid of pressure from the HRC. But the lies which stand up in an American court of law do not stand up before the Lord God, Creator of the marriage covenant which the LGBTQ folks think to redefine. At what point will God say, "I've had it. They have abandoned me, so I will abandon them."?

25

BIBLE REFERENCES PERTAINING TO THE LGBTQ MOVEMENT

It may prove useful to some readers to have key Bible verses pertaining to homosexuality gathered together in this one location.

HOMOSEXUAL BEHAVIOR IS AN ABOMINATION IN GOD'S EYES

"If a man lies with a male as with a woman, both of them have committed an abomination; they shall be put to death, their blood is upon them" (Leviticus 20:13).

"For this reason God gave them up to dishonorable passions. Their women exchanged natural relations for unnatural, and the men likewise gave up natural relations with women and were consumed with passion for one another, men committing shameless acts with men and receiving in their own persons the due penalty for their error" (Romans 1:26–28).

GOD CAN TRANSFORM HOMOSEXUALS

God can transform homosexuals who turn to him, just as he can transform idolaters and alcoholics and thieves.

"Or do you not know that the unrighteous will not inherit the kingdom of God? Do not be deceived: neither the sexually immoral, nor idolaters, nor adulterers, nor men who practice homosexuality, nor thieves, nor the greedy, nor drunkards, nor revilers, nor swindlers will inherit the kingdom of God. And such were some of you. But you were washed, you were sanctified, you were justified in the name of the Lord Jesus Christ and by the Spirit of our God" (1 Corinthians 6:9–11).

Paul said, "And such were some of you," meaning they have been changed by the power of Christ.

SHAME

LGBTQ lifestyles are shameful, but the lesbians and gays and bisexuals and transgenders and queers refuse to be ashamed. Instead, they point the finger and tell those who oppose them *they* are the ones who should be ashamed (a perfect example of psychological transference).

"For it is a shame even to speak of the things that they do in secret ..." (Ephesians 5:12).

"'Were they ashamed when they committed abomination?
No, they were not at all ashamed;
they did not know how to blush.
Therefore they shall fall among those who fall;
at the time that I punish them, they shall be overthrown,' says the LORD"
(Jeremiah 6:15).

LOVE

LGBTQ people invoke love as a justification for their sexual immorality. But Jesus said godly love requires obedience to his commands. In other words, we cannot make up our own rules and still call it love.

> "'He who has my commandments and keeps them, he it is who loves me; and he who loves me will be loved by my Father, and I will love him and manifest myself to him.' Judas (not Iscariot) said to him, 'Lord, how is it that you will manifest yourself to us, and not to the world?' Jesus answered him, 'If a man loves me, he will keep my word, and my Father will love him, and we will come to him and make our home with him. He who does not love me does not keep my words; and the word which you hear is not mine but the Father's who sent me'" (John 14:21–24).

GOD CREATED ONLY TWO SEXES, MALE AND FEMALE

> "So God created man in his own image, in the image of God he created him; male and female he created them" (Genesis 1:27).

MARRIAGE IS BETWEEN ONE MAN AND ONE WOMAN

God's original plan was for one man to marry one woman:

> "Therefore a man leaves his father and his mother and cleaves to his wife, and they become one flesh" (Genesis 2:24).

26

PSALM 78

Testing God

In the message "Introduction to Diversity, Tolerance, Inclusiveness" I quoted a phrase from Psalm 78. I would like to return to Psalm 78 and examine some of its verses in more detail. The psalmist looks back at the many years during which God's people in Israel strayed from God's teaching and worshiped other gods. They had picked liberally from the buffet table of religious inclusiveness. God warned them through his prophets repeatedly, but they persisted in their rebellious attitude.

I will start with the sentence in Psalm 78 containing my original quote about the "deceitful bow":

> "Yet they tested and rebelled against the Most High God, and did not observe his testimonies, but turned away and acted treacherously like their fathers; they twisted like a deceitful bow" (Psalm 78:56–57).

When the psalmist wrote, "they tested" God, he meant they were thinking, "Does God really see? Let's see what we can get away with. Let's see if he takes any action when we go our own way." Aren't those thoughts like the modern atheists who curse God and then say, "Look, nothing happened to me?" More to the point of our message: Isn't that what we do when we say, "God won't care if I dabble in a few other religions and interesting philosophies?" Or when we say, "I won't take sides just yet, I'll wait and see how things pan out." Satan likes it when we say such things. He knows no line of idealistic people holding hands in a show of diversity-tolerance-inclusiveness will be able to stand against the coming wave of destruction.

When the psalmist said they "did not observe his testimonies," his meaning was the fathers did not teach their children to look right and left before crossing the road. Instead, they left their children free to "do their own thing"—exactly what our children are being taught. Our schools encourage our children to run out into the road without looking, if that is "what they want to do." Translated, this means kids are taught: "Choose freely from the buffet table of great ideas, philosophies, ethics, and religions, and whatever seems good to you—live by that. Just remember there is no one 'truth' that applies to everyone."

Is God Tolerant?

The next two verses in Psalm 78 say:

> "For they provoked him to anger with their high places; they moved him to jealousy with their graven images.

> When God heard, he was full of wrath, and he utterly rejected Israel" (Psalm 78:58–59).

In our government system, we have a division of powers. The people who make the laws (the legislators) are different people than the judges who oversee the trials. But in God's kingdom, God is both legislator and judge. God makes the laws and oversees the trials. Human judges may sometimes claim they deliver sentences in a dispassionate way. They may claim they simply follow the letter of the law—a law which was formulated by other people, the legislators. But God is not a dispassionate judge. He is very passionate. He enforces his own laws, not someone else's. The psalmist said God judges with anger, with jealousy, and with wrath. For a human comparison, it would be as though the perpetrator of a murder or a rape were to be judged by the victim's family. The accused man should brace himself for a maximum sentence. And that is the message the psalmist is trying to get across: Those who defy God and God's teaching should brace themselves. Defying

God is not like contradicting another human being. They have defied Almighty God who is Creator and Ruler of the universe.

Is God tolerant? No. When it comes to obedience to his laws, he is passionately intolerant!

Can Any Other Power
Rescue Us?

The Bible tells us God sent warnings to his people Israel over many years, telling them they must obey his commandments. When they refused to listen, God sent the armies of Assyria and Babylon against his people. The foreign armies inflicted much terror and bloodshed, and eventually defeated the people of Israel and took them into exile as captives.

Psalm 78 describes this event:

> "He [God] forsook his dwelling at Shiloh, the tent where he dwelt among men, and delivered his power to captivity, his glory to the hand of the foe" (Psalm 78:60–61).

Shiloh was where God was worshiped when the people of Israel first inhabited the Promised Land. Shiloh was where the Ark of the Covenant was located, kept inside its tent. The Ark and "the tent where [God] dwelt" came under God's special protection. But the people did not worship God in truth. They turned to other gods, other items on the buffet table. Their worship was like a twisted bow. God removed his protection from them and from their place of worship.

If God turns against a nation, all its economic and military power will count as nothing. God has the power to give them over "to the hand of the foe" no matter how strong they may feel, and no matter how much his power may have protected them in the past. There is nothing on the buffet table of inclusiveness that can protect us if God is against us.

When God's Protection is Removed

The author of Psalm 78 goes on to say:

> "He [God] gave his people over to the sword, and vented his wrath on his heritage. Fire devoured their young men, and their maidens had no marriage song.
>
> Their priests fell by the sword, and their widows made no lamentation" (Psalm 78:62–64).

At some point God finally withdrew his protection from his people. There was no escape in 600 B.C., and there will be no escape in our time.

The psalmist records God even punished his "heritage," meaning those who had previously received his blessings and his promises of protection. They are the ones who had been favored by hearing God's word directly from his own mouth, and yet they deserted him.

The "priests" are the watchmen who fell asleep and failed to sound the alarm. They are the shepherds who fed God's flock with false teaching and bland assurances everything would be okay. They are the religious leaders who told their people whatever they wanted to hear.

"The Lord Awoke as from Sleep"

Next the psalmist, with a sudden change of direction, says:

> "Then the LORD awoke as from sleep, like a strong man shouting because of wine.
>
> And he put his adversaries to rout; he put them to everlasting shame" (Psalm 78:65–66).

What is going on now? It seems the adversaries of God's people and of God—Satan and his demons—had their way for a time, but now God is beginning to put his adversaries to rout. But how? The last stanza of the psalm tell us what God did:

> "He rejected the tent of Joseph, he did not choose the tribe of Ephraim; but he chose the tribe of Judah, Mount Zion, which he loves" (Psalm 78:67–68).

At the time the psalmist wrote, two tribes among the people of Israel were striving for supremacy: the tribe of Ephraim (a son of Joseph) and the tribe of Judah. The passage says God chose the tribe of Judah. God determined from the beginning that a special ruler (the Messiah) would come to rule over all God's people, and this ruler should come from the tribe of Judah. This would have come as no surprise to the psalmist's audience, since they knew hundreds of years earlier Jacob had prophesied that the Messiah would come from the descendants of his son Judah. Back in the book of Genesis, when Jacob was blessing his sons, he said of Judah:

"The scepter shall not depart from Judah, nor
the ruler's staff from between his feet, until he
comes to whom it belongs; and to him shall be
the obedience of the peoples" (Genesis 49:10).

It was predestined by God that "the obedience of the peoples" would ultimately come to a descendant of Judah—Jesus of Nazareth. Thus the phrase "the Lord awoke as from sleep" was a prophecy that in its proper time the Messiah, the Savior of Israel, would come.

GOD PROMISED TO SEND A SHEPHERD SAVIOR

That prophecy was made more specific by God's later promises that the Messiah would come from among the descendants of King David, who was himself a descendant of Judah. (And the New Testament tells us Jesus was, in fact, a descendant of David.) In the following verses the psalmist confirms those promises by describing the Messiah as being of the family of David, and as inhabiting a "sanctuary like the high heavens"—meaning a spiritual sanctuary, a sanctuary not made with human hands.

"He built his sanctuary like the high heavens,
like the earth, which he has founded for ever.
He chose David his servant, and took him

from the sheepfolds; from tending the ewes
that had young he brought him to be the
shepherd of Jacob his people, of Israel his
inheritance.

With upright heart he tended them, and guided
them with skillful hand" (Psalm 78:69–72).

Now we're no longer reading about God's wrath. We're no
longer reading about the truck of destruction coming down the
road. We're reading about a shepherd who skillfully protects his
sheep and guides them gently with his hand. And because we
have read to the end of the story (in the New Testament), we
know we are in fact reading about a shepherd who gives his life
for the sheep, a shepherd who gives his life to save them from
Satan's power. We know without this shepherd, the powers of
destruction would consume every single one of us.

The Buffet Table Overturned

Diversity, tolerance, inclusiveness, and equality/equity—the wokeness package—are high-sounding words, but they have become arrows shot from a twisted, deceitful bow. When they are examined closely, we find they all proclaim, "We don't need Jesus and his salvation. We prefer to go our own way."

But how can we refuse such a great salvation, a salvation offered by a God who was willing to give his only Son to die on the cross for us? If there were any other path to salvation, any other viable choice on the big buffet table of inclusiveness, would God have resorted to such a drastic measure? There is only one way, and it excludes all other ways. We know now "that at the name of Jesus every knee [shall] bow, in heaven and on earth and under the earth, and every tongue confess that Jesus Christ is Lord, to the glory of God the Father" (Philippians 2:10–11).

God doesn't want us to be run over by Satan's trucks. He has done his utmost to provide us with a safe path across the busy and dangerous road. Every day he is calling us to bring our thankful hearts to him, to offer our hearts in obedient service to him. And if we will do so, his promise goes beyond mere rescue from disaster. His promise is he will be our God, and we will be his people. His promise is that "the peace of God, which passes all understanding, will keep your hearts and your minds in Christ Jesus" (Philippians 4:7). That is a peace which the religion of diversity-tolerance-inclusiveness—the cult of wokeness—can never provide.

27
TIMES OF STRESS

What is Happening to People?

The apostle Paul made this prediction:

> "But understand this, that in the last days there will come times of stress" (2 Timothy 3:1).

Most of us would say, "Yes, that sounds like my life, all right." We think of stresses at work, health problems, school problems, problems paying bills, and so forth. But Paul identifies a particular sort of stress—stress caused by what is going on inside people. Paul explains the stress he has in mind:

> "For men will be lovers of self, lovers of money, proud, arrogant, abusive, disobedient to their parents, ungrateful, unholy, inhuman, implacable, slanderers, profligates, fierce, haters of good, treacherous, reckless, swollen with conceit, lovers of pleasure rather than lovers of God, holding the form of religion but denying the power of it" (2 Timothy 3:2–5).

We are seeing it happen now. We sometimes hear older people talk about how much "things have changed" in America over the last few decades. What usually goes unsaid is that it is not so much that *things* have changed, as that *people* have changed. We find people who seem to be consumed by Satan. We see people whom we once thought we knew becoming unrecognizable. We can meditate on Paul's list, and check off the items one after another: "proud, arrogant, abusive, disobedient to their parents, ungrateful, unholy, inhuman … lovers of pleasure rather than lovers of God, holding the form of religion but denying the power of it." That last phrase—"holding the form of religion but denying the power of it"—makes it clear Paul does not exclude churchgoers from his list.

HOW TO ESCAPE

We *can't* escape. These things will happen, and Christians will be hated because they put allegiance to Christ first in their lives. A few verses later, Paul tells Timothy:

> "Indeed all who desire to live a godly life in Christ Jesus will be persecuted, while evil men and impostors will go on from bad to worse, deceivers and deceived" (2 Timothy 3:12–13).

We may place our hopes in concepts like freedom of religion and human rights, but those concepts cannot change human hearts. In the end, those who are "deceivers and deceived" will take words and bend them any way they want.

HOW TO SURVIVE: STAND FAST IN THE WORD OF GOD

We cannot escape what will happen, but we can and must survive if we are to be of service to the Lord.

The first basic step in survival is to stand fast in the word of God. Paul told Timothy:

> "All scripture is inspired by God and profitable
> for teaching, for reproof, for correction, and
> for training in righteousness, that the man
> of God may be complete, equipped for every
> good work" (2 Timothy 3:16–17).

Satan hates it when we stand fast in God's word. Satan hates it when God's word has trained us in righteousness, and made us "complete, equipped for every good work." Satan will come against us in any and all the ways described in this book. There is no easy solution for the Christian, but there is a sure solution: stand fast in God's Word and live *in Christ*.

HOW TO SURVIVE: LIVE *IN CHRIST*

We must live in Christ, or we will not survive the times. Jesus told his disciples:

> "I am the vine, you are the branches. He who
> abides in me, and I in him, he it is that bears
> much fruit, for apart from me you can do
> nothing. If a man does not abide in me, he
> is cast forth as a branch and withers; and the

branches are gathered, thrown into the fire and burned" (John 15:5–6).

The whole world needs to hear Jesus' warning: Anyone who does not abide in him will be thrown into the final fire of destruction and burned. On the other hand, anyone who abides in Jesus will not only survive, but will bear much fruit. Yes, it is a matter of survival; but it is more than survival—it is bringing glory to God by bearing fruit. Jesus says, "By this my Father is glorified, that you bear much fruit, and so prove to be my disciples" (John 15:8).

As has been stressed throughout this book, abiding in Christ cannot be separated from obedience to his commandments. "If you keep my commandments, you will abide in my love, just as I have kept my Father's commandments and abide in his love" (John 15:10). When we abide in Christ and obey his commandments, Jesus brings us more than survival, more than avoidance of destruction. He brings us the joy of his presence. "These things I have spoken to you, that my joy may be in you, and that your joy may be full" (John 15:11).

In the days of Nehemiah the governor, Ezra the priest gathered all the people into the central square of Jerusalem and read to them from "the book of the law of Moses which the LORD had given to Israel" (Nehemiah 8:1). He read all morning long, standing on a wooden pulpit, while his assistants helped the people to understand the reading. And "all the people wept when they heard the words of the law" (Nehemiah 8:9). Why would the people weep? Some people yawn when they hear God's word. Others say, "That is an interesting text. I wonder if I can somehow connect it to ancient Babylonian writings, or perhaps find some commonality with Plato's thinking ..."

But the Jews who were gathered before Ezra and Nehemiah wept. They wept first because God's Word testified they had sinned and fallen short of God's requirements. They wept from a sense that by hearing God's Word, they stood in the presence of the Almighty God—the God who was Creator of the universe and to whom they owed their very lives. They wept from a sense of awe that this God had chosen them out of all the peoples of the earth to receive and cherish his words. They must have thought: How can we be worthy of such a gift? They wept from repentant grief, but also from the joy of a grateful heart.

Then Nehemiah and Ezra and the Levites exhorted them, saying, "This day is holy to our LORD; and do not be grieved, for the joy of the LORD is your strength" (Nehemiah 8:10). They were not only hearing God's commands, but they were experiencing the presence of God. They experienced the joy of the Lord—the joy which was their strength.

We can have the same experience. As we read God's word, he draws us near to him—binds us to him—to live in obedience, yes, and to live in his love and joy forever.

A CALL FOR CHRISTIANS TO PRAY

Pray for the destruction of Satan's strongholds: the stronghold of idolatry of science and materialism, which is taught in our schools; the stronghold of infanticide through abortion, which is promoted and paid for by our government; the stronghold of sexual immorality in all the flavors of the LGBTQ movement, which is defended by our courts; and the stronghold of hatred fomented in wokeness and promoted by the media.

Pray for the protection of America's financial system, which is coming under unprecedented stress. (This may not sound like a moral or spiritual issue, but it is part of a plan to destroy our country.)

Pray for the protection of Christians in America and around the world, that they may boldly proclaim God's truth. Pray for the perseverance of the saints.

And give God the praise with thankful hearts, for heartfelt praise is a sacrifice most pleasing to him.

ABOUT THE AUTHOR

Case Olsen has served for many years as a Bible teacher and lay pastor, and has been a close observer of a wide variety of churches and missions. People who have heard his teaching have repeatedly told him, "You need to publish that and get it out there"—so here it is. Case has a BA in Religious Studies from Yale, and an MS in Computer Science from Queens College, City University of New York.

INDEX

F

G

H

I

R

S

W

Y

BIBLE REFERENCES